Basic Fly Tying
in Pictures

Ted Andrews
Basic Fly Tying in Pictures

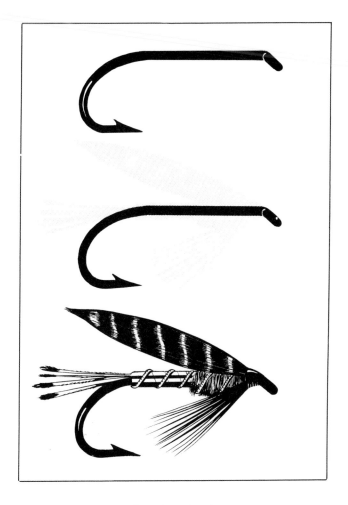

Stanley Paul
London Melbourne Sydney Auckland Johannesburg

Stanley Paul & Co. Ltd

An imprint of the Hutchinson Publishing Group

17–21 Conway Street, London W1P 6JD

Hutchinson Group (Australia) Pty Ltd
30–32 Cremorne Street, Richmond South, Victoria 3121
PO Box 151, Broadway, New South Wales 2007

Hutchinson Group (NZ) Ltd
32–34 View Road, PO Box 40–086, Glenfield, Auckland 10

Hutchinson Group (SA) (Pty) Ltd
PO Box 337, Bergvlei 2012, South Africa

First published 1983
© Ted Andrews 1983

Set in Plantin by
D.P. Media Limited, Hitchin, Hertfordshire

Printed in Great Britain by The Anchor Press Ltd
and bound by Wm Brendon & Son Ltd,
both of Tiptree, Essex

British Library Cataloguing in Publication Data
Andrews, Ted
  Basic fly-tying in pictures.
  1. Fly tying – Pictorial works
  I. Title
  688.7′912   SH451

ISBN 0 09 149891 0

Contents

Acknowledgements

I should like to take the opportunity of saying thank you to a number of people who have helped me greatly in the preparation of 'Flystrip' and ultimately this book. First, to Fred J. Taylor, sportsman, for his help and encouragement with my work and for the example set to me and countless other anglers through his writings over the years. To Donald Downs for his friendship, encouragement, advice and for the foreword for this book. To Taff Price of John Veniard Limited who, despite running a successful flydressing business, found time to answer my queries. And a special thank you to James Nice of Sidmouth for his truly expert advice and for supplying the hackle feathers to be seen on the back cover of this book.

Lastly, to Bob, Malcolm, Paul, Joe and Brian, my fishing companions, whose friendship and enthusiasm for flyfishing I am privileged to share.

Foreword

When I first met Ted Andrews some eleven years ago, I was much impressed by his capabilities as an angler, flydresser and cartoonist. While this latter attribute may seem of little angling relevance, it has been a most important factor in the shaping of this book. It takes remarkably acute observation and skill to get the likeness of a face or an action with the fewest number of lines, or to make some salient point in a drawing with brevity. Such rapid sketches of course are no accidents, but rely on Ted's underlying ability to be a most meticulous draughtsman.

In this book he puts together his knowledge, experience and drawing abilities to show us simple flies and their dressings. They are taken from a selection that he has himself tied and fished with many times; for the large part they are simple, but very effective patterns, employing straightforward techniques in their manufacture. We are taken through the stages of their dressing with a few pertinent drawings to show the vital steps leading from bare hook to finished fly. Simplicity is Ted's keynote, and he gives us a crisp small volume, uncluttered by too many words or by a complexity of sketches – a boon to the practical man or woman who wishes a clear quick reference while at the tying table.

He has written this book with the object of helping those many anglers who wish to take that great step towards the supreme satisfaction of knowing that every fish that they land has been taken on a fly that they have tied themselves.

Donald Downs

Introduction

Some time ago I produced a feature on basic flydressing for the weekly paper *Anglers Mail*. Despite my belief that it would have only a limited run, to my surprise the series was published over a two-and-a-half-year period and prompted much welcome correspondence. Its modest success can only be attributed to the tremendous interest in flydressing generated by the upsurge of popularity of stillwater trout fishing in recent years.

This book, and indeed the features that preceded it, does not set out to be an exhaustive treatise on flydressing methods, but rather an introduction to some basic techniques, coupled with a selection of proven trout fly patterns. I sincerely hope that through these pages the reader will feel prompted to begin a truly fascinating hobby, that will add an enormously satisfying dimension to the hugely enjoyable sport of flyfishing.

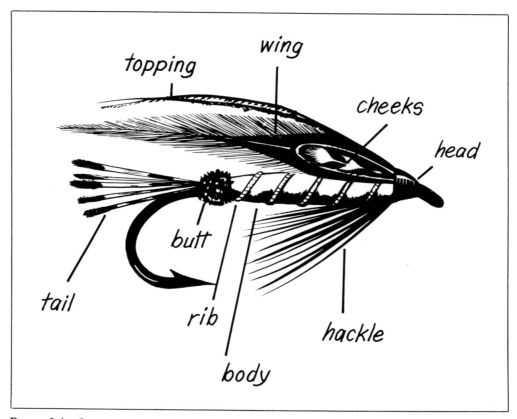

Parts of the fly

The Flies We Tie

In this chapter the reader will find examples of some of the main types of trout flies which he can learn to tie in the pages that follow.

Dry flies

Dry flies are fished on the surface. They are usually dressed on fine wire hooks (to assist floating) with an upturned eye.

Hackled dry fly

The traditional hackled dry fly has a stiff-fibred cock hackle. This represents the beating wings of a natural insect and supports the fly on the water surface. A further refinement is the addition of wings made from matched slips of feathers taken from the wing quills of such birds as the starling and blackbird.

HACKLED
DRY FLY

Winged dry fly

The pair (or two pairs) of wings may be tied in the upright position or 'advanced' (which means the wings slope forward over the eye).

WINGED
DRY FLY

Spent wing dry fly

This shows a mayfly with its wings in the 'spent' position – tied flat to the water. Spent wings are normally made from hackle tips, although bunches of feather fibre and hair are sometimes used.

SPENT WING
MAYFLY

Wet flies

Wet flies are fished below the surface. Those depicted below, and popular with generations of trout fishermen, are traditional winged wet flies. Although they are not precise copies of natural insects they catch a respectable proportion of stillwater trout.

In contrast to the winged fly, the Black and Peacock Spider is typical of the simple hackled wet fly.

Wet or dry flies with the hackle wound the length of the hook shank are described as being 'palmered', and the Invicta and Zulu are among the most popular.

MALLARD AND CLARET

ZULU

PETER ROSS

INVICTA

BUTCHER

HACKLED
WET FLY

Nymphs

The word 'nymph' is used to describe the larval stage of an insect which lives and feeds beneath the surface of the water prior to hatching into an adult fly. Nymph patterns are fished beneath the surface of the water or in the surface film.

MIDGE PUPA

DRAGON FLY NYMPH

Artificial nymphs may be accurate copies of a real insect (above). Alternatively, they may suggest general shape and coloration, as in the Amber Nymph and Chomper patterns.

AMBER NYMPH

CHOMPER

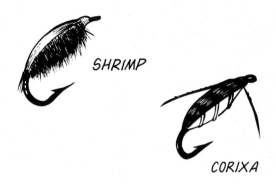

SHRIMP

CORIXA

The Corixa and Shrimp, although not nymphs in the strictest sense of the word (being fully developed creatures in their own right), are generally grouped under the heading nymph and fished in the same way.

Lures

Lures are normally tied on long shank hooks to represent small fish such as sticklebacks, minnows and fry.

Some have a wing formed from marabou, a wonderfully soft feather material which 'works' attractively when the fly is retrieved.

SWEENY TODD

A lure may have wings made from a pair of matched hackle feathers. Patterns dressed this way are referred to as having whole feather or streamer wings.

Flies tied with two or more hooks joined together one behind the other are known as tandems. Monofilament line connects the two hooks, although plastic-covered wire is sometimes used for this purpose.

The Tools for the Job

The amateur dresser needs few tools. Most important is the vice of which there are two types – the collet (left) and lever. Choose a model that will accommodate a variety of hook sizes.

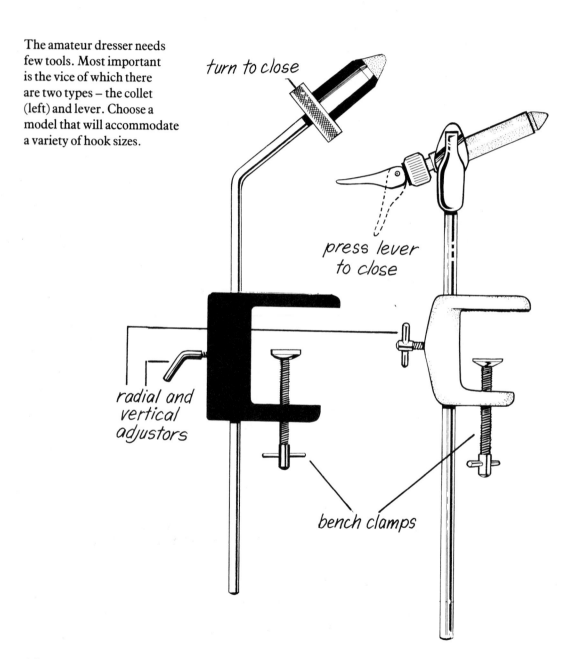

turn to close

press lever to close

radial and vertical adjustors

bench clamps

Two pairs of scissors are required, one of which should have flat, slim blades with a sharp point for delicate work.
The other pair needs to be more robust, for jobs like cutting quills and tinsels.

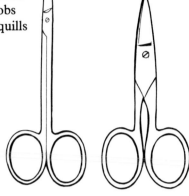

The dubbing needle is used for picking out fur and feather, but also may be used as an applicator for varnish and clearing the hook eye.

Beeswax is sold in cake and liquid form and is used for coating the tying silk before dressing.

A pair of pointed tweezers is a useful item to add to your kit.

The spigot bobbin holder serves two functions. It dispenses silk from the reel via the tube and acts as a weight to hold the dressings in place during tying, leaving the hands free.

There are many preparations for coating the head of the fly, but a bottle of clear nail varnish serves the purpose.

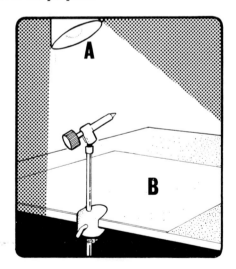

Hackle pliers are designed to hold the hackle while it is being wound. Buy two pairs, one large, one small.

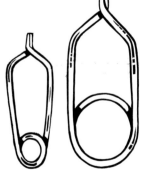

A. A good source of light is vital and an angle-poise type lamp is ideal.
B. A piece of white paper or card placed beneath the vice provides a clear background against which to work.

Hooks

Fly hooks are manufactured in various styles and patterns to suit the type of fly that you want to tie. Some have off-set points, others have up- or down-turned eyes, and even the diameter of the wire they are made from can differ from maker to maker.

making your first purchase, buy multiples of 100 – it is the best way to buy them.

Hooks are numbered according to their size. The higher the number the smaller the hook. A small dry fly hook would normally be a size 14 or 16 whereas a large lure hook might be a size 8.

Useful dry fly sizes (normally up-eyed) are 10, 12, 14, 16 and 18, with wet flies being tied right through the scale. Generally, English hook manufacturers follow what is known as the Redditch scale, which runs from a size 18 up to a no. 1. Nowadays, odd-numbered hooks are becoming scarcer and, in the main, only even sizes are being made.

The pattern of fly you want to tie will determine the length of the hook you should buy.

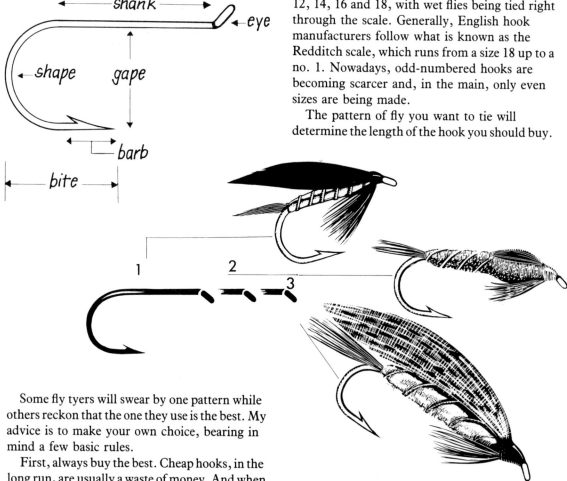

Some fly tyers will swear by one pattern while others reckon that the one they use is the best. My advice is to make your own choice, bearing in mind a few basic rules.

First, always buy the best. Cheap hooks, in the long run, are usually a waste of money. And when

Hook 1 (opposite left) is a standard length down-eyed hook which is used for traditional wet fly patterns. Hook 2 has a slightly longer shank which is used for tying nymphs. Pattern 3 has the longest shank and is used for making lures.

Hook bends generally come in three different patterns – roundbend, sproat and Limerick.

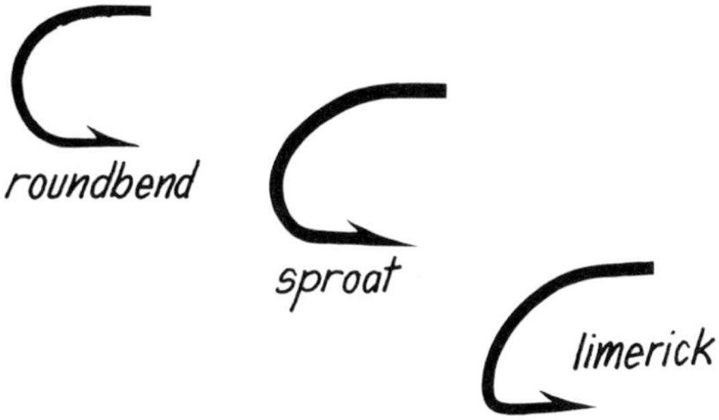

Eyes are also bent three different ways – up-eyed (dry fly), down-eyed (wet fly) and straight-eyed.

up-eyed   down-eyed   straight-eyed

Whether to choose a hook with a straight or off-set point (reversed or kirbed) is basically a matter of personal preference.

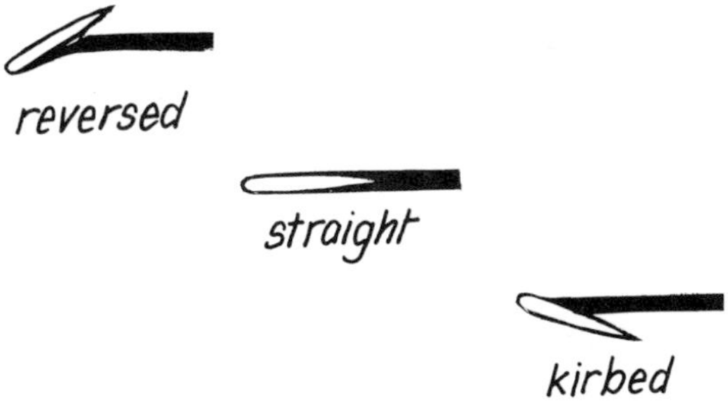

roundbend

sproat

limerick

reversed

straight

kirbed

Materials in Brief

The range of materials available for dressing flies is vast, but it is not vital to possess scores of feathers and boxes of furs, silks and tinsels in order to get started.

Some of the deadliest flies in use today rely on only two or three simple components in their construction. For example, the late Frank Sawyer's masterpiece – the Pheasant Tail Nymph – doesn't even incorporate silk.

One of the easiest ways to begin this fascinating hobby is to obtain one of the many starter kits offered by fly dressing stockists. They contain a variety of materials which will suit the beginner's needs. Alternatively, buy only what you know you need to tie the patterns with which you start your fly tying, and add to the materials as you move onto new patterns.

Silk

Comes in a variety of colours and shades. Used for attaching materials to the hook shank and forming bodies of certain patterns. Pre-waxed and extra fine silks are available but the standard 'Gossamer' type suits most needs.

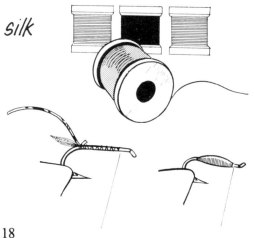

Floss

Used for bodies and, in some patterns, underbodies of a great many flies. A ribbon-type material available in a wide range of colours including fluorescent.

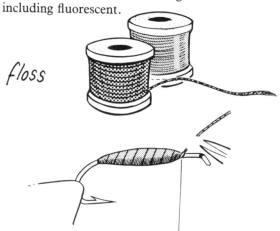

Tinsels

A metallic ribbon in gold and silver used to form shiny bodies and ribs of many fly patterns. Flat tinsels are used to make flies such as Butcher, Priest and Wickham's Fancy. Oval tinsel is used for ribbing. For small patterns a plain wire in gold and silver is available for ribbing. Lurex, the brand name for a shiny plastic-based body material, will not tarnish. It is available in ten colours as well as gold and silver.

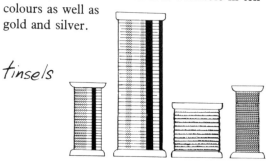

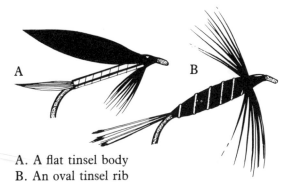

A. A flat tinsel body
B. An oval tinsel rib

Herls
Taken from whole feathers. Peacock, heron, ostrich, swan, goose, cock pheasant (tail) and turkey herls all make excellent fly bodies.

Fur
Mole, rabbit, hare and seal are just a few of the creatures that provide fur in natural or dyed form for fly dressing. It is spun between thumb and fore finger onto the silk and then wound along the hook shank, to form the body. This technique is known as dubbing.

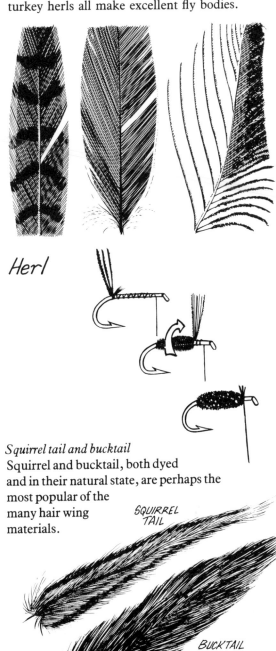

Herl

Fur

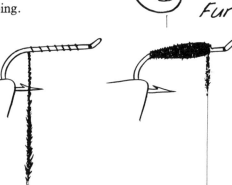

Wool
A variety of colours and textures make wool a fine material for fly bodies.

Wool

Chenille
A soft, fluffy, floss-type material used to make the bodies of lures and some of the larger nymphs.

Squirrel tail and bucktail
Squirrel and bucktail, both dyed and in their natural state, are perhaps the most popular of the many hair wing materials.

SQUIRREL TAIL

BUCKTAIL

Chenille

19

Basic Steps

Before tying your first fly, it is a good idea to practise attaching the silk to the hook shank, running the silk evenly up and down, and finishing off with the whip finish knot.

Soon your hands will respond to working with delicate materials and you will have more confidence.

1. To start with choose a large hook. Place it in the vice so that the bend and point are covered by the jaws. Take care not to tighten the chuck too tightly as this may damage the point and barb.

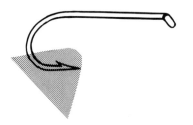

2. Next put a spool of silk in your bobbin holder. Then draw off about 12 inches, pull it quickly but lightly over your tablet of beeswax. The wax makes the silk tacky and helps to stop it rotting.

3. Now wind 10 inches of silk back onto the reel and place the remaining 2 inches behind the hook and hold it with the left hand.

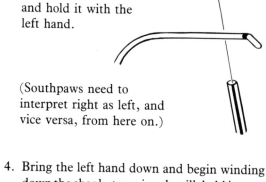

(Southpaws need to interpret right as left, and vice versa, from here on.)

4. Bring the left hand down and begin winding down the shank, trapping the silk held in your hand.

5. After two or three turns, pause to trim off the waste silk. Continue down to the bend with even turns of the silk.

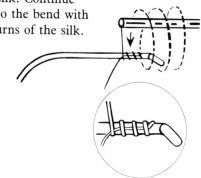

6. Run the silk back up to the eye and tie the whip finish by forming a loop of silk.

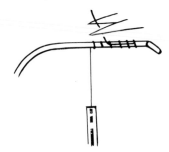

7. Now, by rolling two fingers inside the loop and over the eye of the hook, trap the length of silk which runs parallel to the shank.

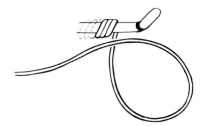

8. Repeat this motion three or four times.

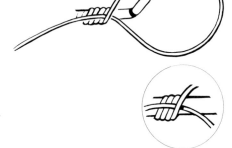

9. Although a specialist tool is available (called, not surprisingly, a whip finish tool), I would recommend mastering the knot with your fingers. Some fly dressers use the more simple half-hitch, but I feel the whip finish is far safer.

10. Pull tight and trim off waste silk.

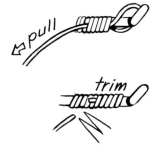

Chompers for Starters

Dick Walker's excellent Chompers pattern has much to recommend it, for not only is it perhaps the simplest of patterns for the newcomer to attempt but, tied in a variety of colours and sizes, it has the added advantage of representing a variety of natural creatures found in stillwaters. Colour combinations include: green back, white body; black back and body; brown back, green body.

Basic materials are:
Hook: DE 8–14
Silk: to match body colour
Body: two or three strands of ostrich herl
Back: raffene

1. Run the waxed tying silk down to the bend and tie in a length of raffene (synthetic raffia). Follow this with two or three lengths of ostrich herl.

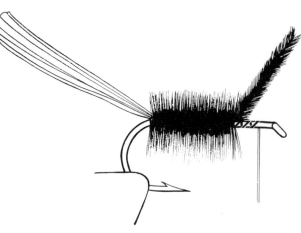

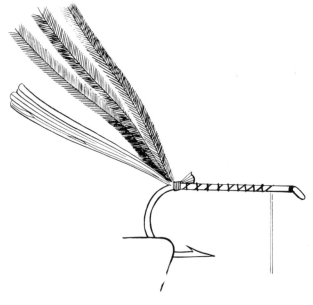

2. Take the silk back to the eye and then, by twisting the herls anticlockwise, make a rope which is then wound up the shank to the eye. Tie it in and trim off waste.

3. Moisten the finger and thumb with saliva and thoroughly dampen the raffene. Stretch the raffene over the back and tie it in at the head. Trim off waste.

4. With the silk, build up a neat head and complete the fly with a whip finish. Varnish the head of the fly but not the raffene back.

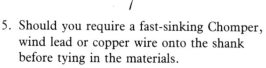

5. Should you require a fast-sinking Chomper, wind lead or copper wire onto the shank before tying in the materials.

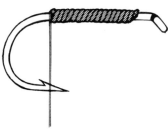

Corixa

Hook: DE 10–14
Silk: black
Body: white floss
Rib: oval silver tinsel
Back or wing cases: a bunch of cock pheasant tail fibres
Legs: two cock pheasant tail fibres tied in by the tips and trimmed to length

1. Wax the tying silk and run it down to the bend. Catch in by the tips a bunch of cock pheasant tail fibres, followed by a length of oval silver tinsel and then a length of white floss.

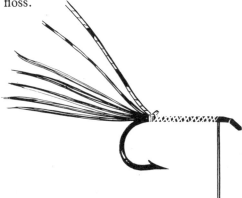

2. Take the silk back to near the eye. Build up a fattish body with floss and rib it neatly with the tinsel.

3. Gather the pheasant tail fibres together and pull them forward over the floss and secure them with turns of silk behind the eye. Trim off waste herl.

4. A pair of pheasant tail fibres are now tied in behind the eye to represent the paddlelike legs of the Corixa. Build up a neat head with turns of silk and whip finish. To make this pattern a little more durable I generally varnish the whole fly, including the paddles.

5. The finished Corixa.

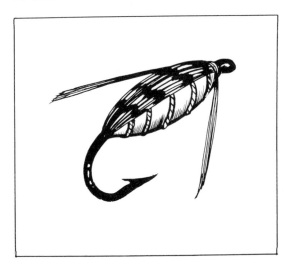

Suede Chenille Sedge Pupa

Hook: DE 10–14 standard length and long shank may be used
Silk: tan
Body: green suede chenille
Thorax: three fibres of chestnut brown ostrich herl
Antennae: a doubled length of the tying silk trimmed to length

1. Cut a length of suede chenille and strip away the fluffy fibres at one end, exposing the central core of the material. Run the waxed tying silk down the shank and tie in the chenille by its core at the point shown on the drawing.

2. Return the silk up the hook shank and then wind up the chenille into a neat body. Tie off and trim waste.
   Next tie in three fibres of chestnut brown ostrich herl.

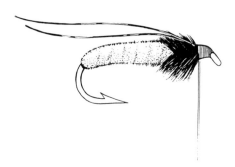

3. Spin the ostrich herl between finger and thumb into a rope and wind it forward to a point a little way behind the eye. Tie off and trim.

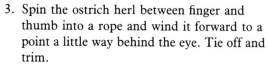

4. A double length of silk is now tied in behind the eye to represent trailing antennae. Build up a large head with turns of silk, whip finish and varnish.

Lastly place a drop of varnish on your forefinger and work it into the silk antennae.

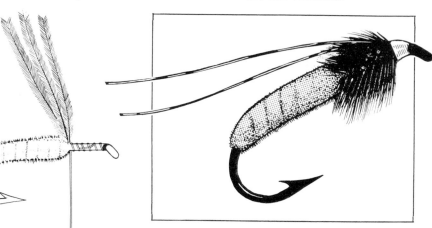

Marabou Bloodworm

Taff Price is, in my opinion, one of the foremost innovative fly dressers presently at work in this country. A director of a leading firm of fly-dressing suppliers, Taff has at his disposal a wealth of materials but produces effective patterns, simple to dress, from materials that are readily available. His Marabou Bloodworm pattern illustrates these points well.

Hook: LS 12–14
Silk: crimson
Tail: red marabou
Body: red floss
Rib: fluorescent red silk
Head: peacock herl

1. Take the tying silk down to the bend and there tie in a tuft of red marabou.

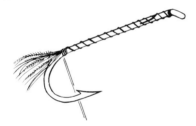

2. Next the ribbing of fluorescent silk is tied in, followed by a length of red floss.

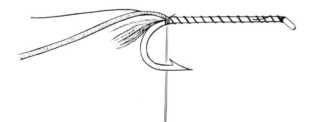

3. The floss is now wound up the hook shank so as to produce an undulating segmented effect. Tie off and trim waste floss. The body is then ribbed with the fluorescent silk.

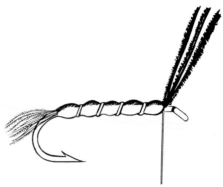

4. Three peacock herls are tied in at the position shown on the drawing and wound into a neat head. Tie off and trim waste herl. Whip finish and varnish.

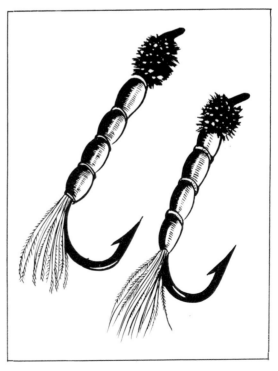

Hatching Midge Pupa

Tie the Midge Pupa in a wide variety of colours which should include black, buff, crimson, green and orange.

Hook: DE or SE 8–14
Silk: black
Body: black floss
Rib: flat silver tinsel or Lurex
Thorax: two or three fibres of peacock herl
Breathing tubes: small tufts of white marabou

1. Starting behind the eye, take the waxed tying silk down the shank and well round the bend of the hook. Catch in a small tuft of white marabou.

2. Follow this with a length of flat silver tinsel or Lurex and then a length of black floss. Return the tying silk to the point shown.

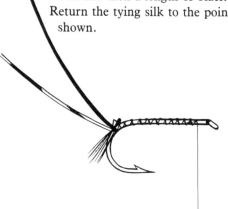

3. Wind the floss up the shank into a tapered shape and tie it in as shown. Trim off waste and follow up with the tinsel rib in neat, even turns. Tie in and trim off waste.

4. Tie in a further tuft of white marabou and then two or three strands of peacock herl.

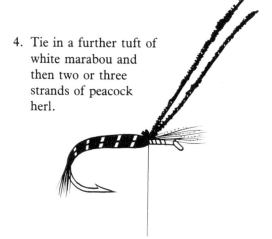

5. Make a rope of the herl by twisting it together anticlockwise, then wind round the hook shank two or three times to form the thorax. Tie in and trim off waste. Lift the marabou tuft and make a neat head with the tying silk. Complete with a whip finish and then varnish.

trim

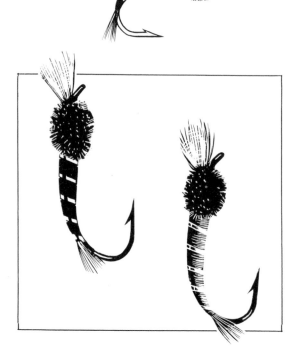

26

Sawyer's Pheasant Tail Nymph

This fly is unique in that no tying silk is used. Fine copper wire is wound round the hook shank to form the weighted body and to tie in the fibres. The copper wire should be reddish brown and slightly thicker than a human hair.

Hook: DE 14–16
Body: fine copper wire overwound with pheasant tail fibres.

1. Start the copper wire behind the eye and wind down the shank, building up a nymph shape with a pronounced thorax.

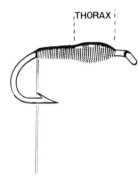

2. Catch in four cock pheasant tail fibres leaving the tips extended about one eighth of an inch beyond the bend to form the tail. With thumb and forefinger twist wire and herls together into a rope (see diagram 2a).

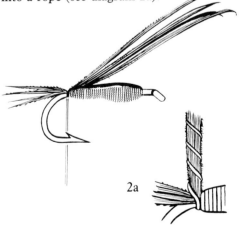

2a

3. Wind the rope forward up the shank to the eye to cover completely the copper underbody. Separate the copper from the herls behind the eye and secure them with a couple of turns of wire.

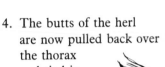
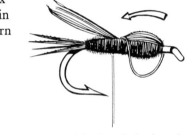

4. The butts of the herl are now pulled back over the thorax and tied in with a turn of wire.

5. Repeat the operation, this time bringing the herls forward toward the eye where they are tied down. Trim off the waste herl and build up a small head with turns of wire. Whip finish and varnish.

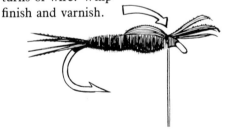

Dubbing

Many 'recipes' for trout flies call for a dubbed body. This is made using wool or fur, which is spun onto the tying silk and then wound up the shank of the hook to form the body of the fly. The fur fibres of seal, rabbit and hare are among the most popular of a great many materials used for dubbing.

1. Run the waxed tying silk down the bend of the hook – choose a large one, say size 8, for practice purposes. Now separate the fur fibres between your forefinger and thumb and spread a thin layer of fur over the ball of your forefinger.

2. Transfer the fur to the tying silk and spin it on with a rolling action of the thumb and forefinger. The rolling action must go in one direction only.

2a. The fur should completely cover the tying silk.

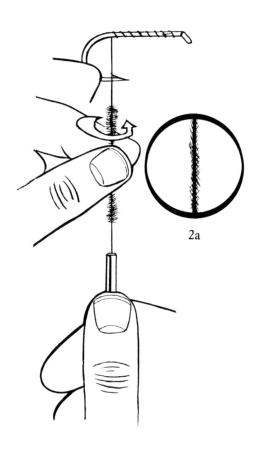

2a

3. Further spinnings of fur may be added until you judge that there is enough to form the body.

4. Now wind the silk up the shank in even turns and tie in to complete.

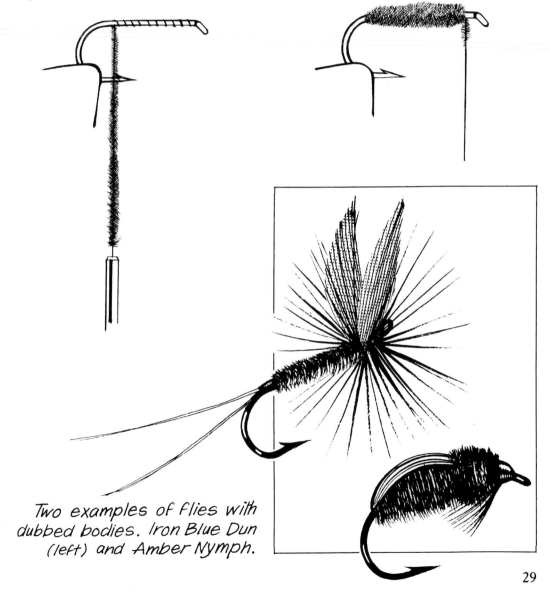

Two examples of flies with dubbed bodies. Iron Blue Dun (left) and Amber Nymph.

Cove's Pheasant Tail

Arthur Cove's Pheasant Tail contains what are perhaps the basic ingredients of a perfect fly. It is, first, a superb deceiver of stillwater trout, second, simple to dress, and third, made from materials that are inexpensive and easy to obtain.

Hook: DE 6–8–10
Silk: brown
Rib: copper wire
Body: three or four fibres of cock pheasant tail
Thorax: dubbed rabbit or hare's fur

1. Take the waxed brown tying silk down the shank and round the bend to the point shown on the drawing. For the rib, tie in a length of copper wire followed by three or four fibres of cock pheasant for the body.

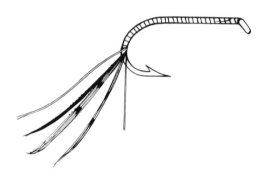

2. Spin the pheasant tail fibres between finger and thumb into a rope and then wind it forward and tie off at the point shown. The body is now neatly ribbed with even spirals of copper wire. Tie off the wire and trim waste.

3. The silk is now dubbed with natural rabbit or hare's fur.

4. Wind the dubbed silk into a neat ball-shaped thorax. Take a few turns of silk behind the eye, and complete with a varnished whip finish.

Drawing A shows a pheasant tail tied on a standard hook.

Drawing B illustrates the same pattern tied on a Yorkshire sedge hook – my own preference for this fly.

A   B

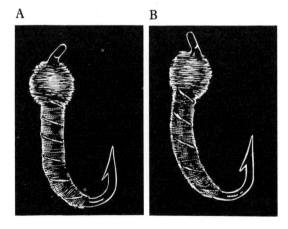

Winding a Hackle

Feathers taken from the neck of the domestic chicken are used to make the hackles of both dry and wet flies.

Cock hackle
The cock bird provides the stiff steely hackle fibres which support the dry fly on the surface.

Hen hackle
Hackles taken from the hen bird are softer. They are used for making wet flies.

1. Before tying in the hackle, strip away the downy fibres at the butt end of the feather. Trim the quill with scissors leaving about one eighth of an inch spare.

2. With a figure-of-eight winding, tie in the feather with the shiny side facing the eye of the hook. Wind the silk back towards the bend of the hook lashing down the remainder of the quill.

3. Attach a pair of hackle pliers to the tip of the feather and begin to wind the feather back towards the bend.

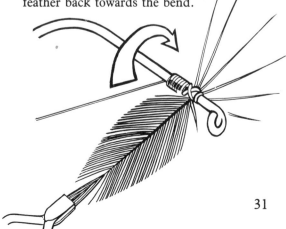

4. After four or five turns, tie in the hackle with the silk and trim off the waste feather.

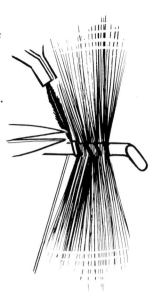

5. To finish, wind the silk carefully back through the hackle and build up the head with turns of silk. Use the whip finish to complete the hackle. Winding hackles is not difficult – it simply requires practice.

Some patterns incorporate a 'false hackle' which is simply a bunch of fibres taken usually from a cock or hen hackle feather and tied in as illustrated.

False hackle

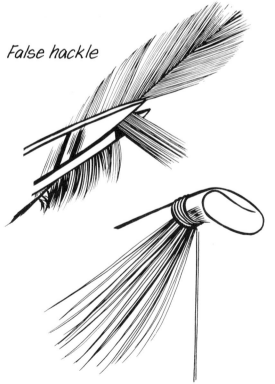

The best way of obtaining a ready supply of hackle feathers is to purchase a selection of capes. A cape is the neck section of skin taken from the domestic chicken (both cock and hen) to which are attached a host of hackle feathers of varying size. Your choice of colours and shades will be determined by the flies you dress but I suggest the following capes would be useful to begin your collection: black cock, black hen, ginger, natural red, badger (a white feather with a black centre) and finally a dyed medium olive. The back cover of this book shows a variety of hackle feathers in common use.

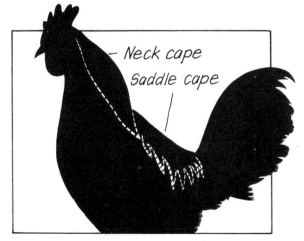

Neck cape
Saddle cape

Black and Peacock Spider

Without doubt this is one of the most popular wet fly patterns in use today, and one that can be relied upon to take trout from the first day of the season to the last.

Hook: DE 8–14 standard length
Silk: black
Underbody: black floss
Body: four fibres of peacock herl
Hackle: soft black hen

1. Leaving a little space behind the eye, wind the silk down to the bend.

2. Catch in four fibres of peacock herl followed by a length of black floss. Return the tying silk to the eye.

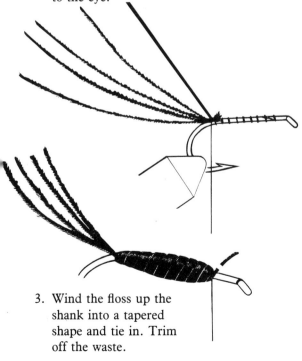

3. Wind the floss up the shank into a tapered shape and tie in. Trim off the waste.

4. Next, twist the peacock fibres into a 'rope' and wind up the hook shank. Tie in and trim off the waste.

5. Finally tie in and wind a soft black hen hackle, two turns only. Trim off waste, whip finish and varnish.

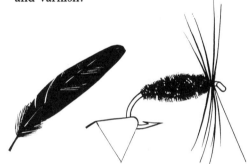

6. Should you require a fast-sinking fly, substitute the black floss underbody with lead or copper wire.

Black Pennel

The Black Pennel is a traditional lake pattern which is straightforward to tie and a proven killer of trout.

Hook: DE 8–14
Silk: black
Tail: three or four fibres of golden pheasant tippet (illustrated above)
Rib: fine silver oval tinsel or wire
Body: black floss
Hackle: black hen

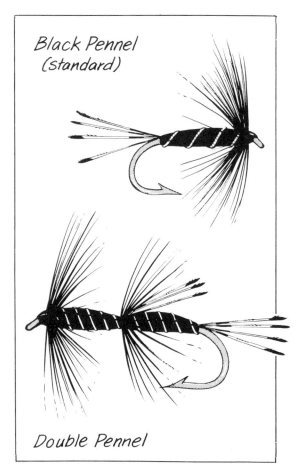

Black Pennel
(standard)

Double Pennel

1. Run the waxed tying silk down to the bend and tie in three or four fibres of golden pheasant tippet for the tail. A length of silver tinsel or wire is added, followed by a length of black floss.

2. Return the silk to the eye and wind the floss up the shank into a slim tapering body. Rib the body evenly with the silver tinsel or wire.

3. A soft black hen hackle feather is now tied in and wound. I would recommend a maximum of two turns only.

With turns of silk, make a neat head, whip finish and varnish.

While fishing Barn Elms on one occasion I was shown an interesting variation of this pattern by New Malden angler Bob Mitchell. Two pennels are simply tied one behind the other on a size 8 long shank lure hook. Bob tells me that this fly has worked well for him, particularly at the beginning of the season.

34

Red Palmer

A simple pattern to dress, the Palmer style of fly has been popular for many years. The dressing here is for the red version, but green and black are also useful colours.

Hook: DE 8–14
Silk: red
Body: red seal's fur
Hackle: natural red cock hackle feather
Rib: oval gold tinsel or fine gold wire

1. Run the waxed tying silk down to the hook bend and tie in a length of fine oval tinsel or gold wire.

2. Dub the body material onto the silk and wind up the shank to form a tapered body. Tie in a large natural red cock hackle feather.

3. Wind the hackle feather the length of the body and trap the last turn with the tinsel or gold wire. Trim the surplus tip of the hackle feather.

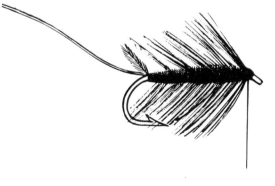

4. Take the tinsel or gold wire back up the hook shank, crossing the turns of hackle. Tie in the rib at the head with the tying silk. Trim off surplus rib, whip finish and varnish.

Woolly Worm

The Woolly Worm may be tied in a variety of colours, green, brown and yellow being most popular.

Hook: DE 8–14
Silk: to match body colour
Tail: a tuft of red wool
Hackle: grizzle cock
Body: chenille

1. Starting behind the eye, take the waxed tying silk down to the bend and there tie in a tuft of red wool for the tail.
   Now tie in a grizzle cock hackle (a white feather barred with black).

2. Strip away the fluffy fibres from a short length of chenille, exposing a tippet of the central core of the material.
   The chenille is now tied in by the exposed core in front of the hackle feather.
   Return the silk to the eye.

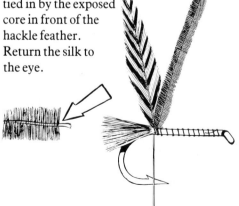

3. Wind the chenille up the shank in touching turns, tie off behind the eye and trim waste. The hackle is now wound in wide even turns over the chenille body. Trap the hackle tip with a couple of turns of silk behind the eye and trim waste feather. Build up the head with turns of silk, whip finish and varnish.

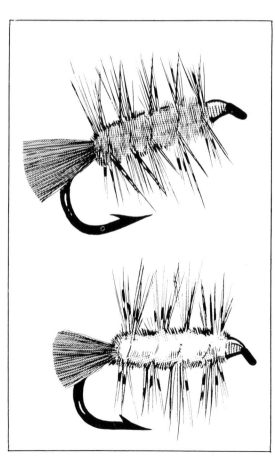

Partridge and Orange

It will be a comfort to the flydressing newcomer to be reminded that some of the most effective patterns are simple to dress. The Partridge and Orange, which requires the minimum of materials, illustrates this point well.

Hook: DE 8–14
Silk: orange
Body: orange floss, or turns of tying silk, in the smaller hook sizes
Hackle: brown partridge

1. Start the waxed tying silk a little way behind the eye and take it down to the bend, then catch in a length of orange floss. Return the silk to the eye and wind up a neat body with the floss.

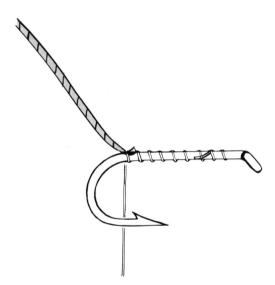

2. Tie off the floss and trim off the excess. Next tie in a brown partridge feather and wind a neat hackle. Take the silk through the hackle and build up a small head with turns of silk, whip finish and varnish.

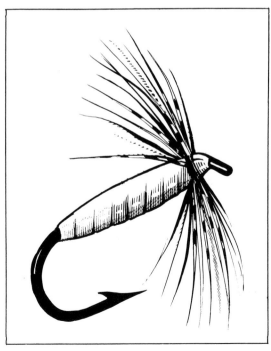

Leaded Flies

It is sometimes necessary to weight wet flies to counteract the current in a stream, or to present a fly quickly to a cruising stillwater fish that might be feeding a couple of feet below the surface.

Although fly fishermen talk of 'leaded flies', this is a generalization referring to any pattern that has an underbody constructed from lead wire, thin lead sheeting, copper or even fuse wire. The object is to give added ballast.

1–2. Shows a hook with open turns of silk taken down to the bend. The silk will give a key to the lead wire which is then wound on in a tapered shape as in No. 2. A few turns of silk may then be taken back over the wire to make it doubly secure. A coat of varnish at this stage is a further refinement.

3–4. Lead sheeting is cut into thin strips and wound onto the hook shank. Good quality wine bottles have a wrapping of lead to cover the corks which is ideal for fly tying purposes. Empty oil paint tubes are also extremely good.

3.

1.

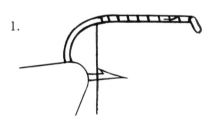

2.

4.

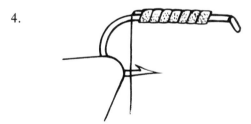

5–6. This is an ingenious method devised by
Dick Walker of making the fly fish hook
point upwards. Strips of lead are bound to
the top of the hook shank one on top of the
other. The dressing is then completed in
the normal way, producing a fly that is
extremely useful when fishing over a weedy
lake or river bottom.

5.

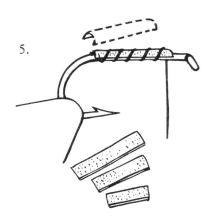

6.

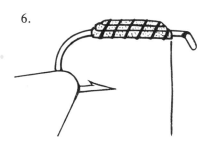

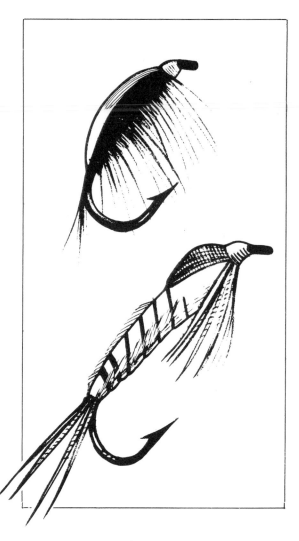

Leaded Shrimp

Hook: DE 8–12
Silk: olive
Body: lead wire
Back: fluorescent green wool (lime)
Underbody: lead wire

1. Begin by cutting a 4-inch length of fluorescent green wool. With a dubbing needle, shred the wool throughout its length. This done, place it to one side.

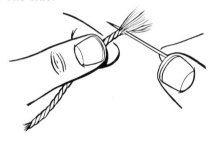

2. The hook is now bound with lead wire and a generous coat of varnish laid over the winding.

3. While the varnish is still wet, start the tying silk behind the eye and take it in tight turns down to the bend. Tie in the shredded wool as shown.

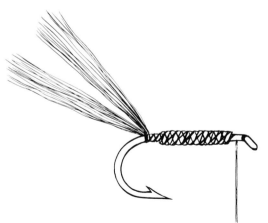

4. Return the silk back to the eye and there tie in a length of fluorescent green wool.

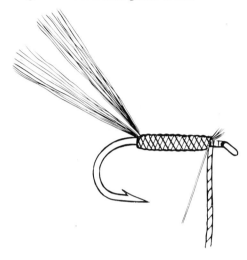

5. Wind the wool down to the bend and then return it to the eye, building up a fat body. Tie off and trim waste.

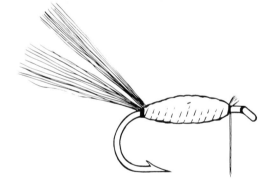

6. With the dubbing needle, separate a few wool fibres for a tail, gather the remainder and stretch over the back of the fly. Secure with a couple of turns of silk. Separate a few more fibres with the dubbing needle and trim away the remainder. Build up a head with turns of silk. Whip finish and varnish.

7. Remove the fly from the vice and with a scalpel or razor blade, slightly score along the belly of the fly. The dubbing needle is now used to tease down the body material, copying the legs of the natural shrimp.

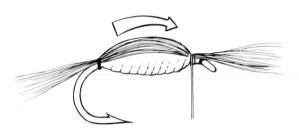

Wet Fly Wings

There are several methods of winging the traditional wet fly, although the principle is the same for all of them. Two matching slips of feather are pulled down vertically onto the hook shank by a loop formed with the tying silk. This is not very difficult, but it requires practice. I would advise tying at least half a dozen pairs of wings before embarking on a finished fly.

Wings are tied from wing, breast and tail feathers of a variety of birds. Those in my drawing show quill feathers – white tip blue mallard – which form the wings of the popular Butcher pattern.

1. A pair of quill feathers is taken from left and right wings.

2. With a dubbing needle, select a slip of feather approximately three-sixteenths of an inch wide and cut it from the quill.

3. Do the same with the other feather to form two matched slips. Looking edgewise it will be noticed that each one has a natural curve which helps when the wing is tied in.

4. Fix a down-eyed hook in the vice and start with the waxed silk behind the eye, winding down the shank for four or five touching turns. This provides a 'bed' of silk upon which the wings will sit.

5. Match the two slips of feather together (curving inwards, as shown in No. 3) and then with the finger and thumb of the left hand, offer them up to the hook.

6. Pinching the two slips together and down onto the hook shank, take the silk up between the thumb and the wing slip nearest you, over the wing and hook shank and then down between the forefinger and opposite wing slip. Bring the silk up again between the thumb and nearest wing slip and hold it there as shown.

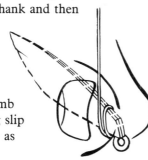

The following points are essential to satisfactory tying of wet fly wings:

Four or five turns of silk must be wound onto the hook shank behind the eye; wings will not sit properly on a bare hook.

The forefinger and thumb holding the wings must not be moved during the tying process.

The wings must be pinched tightly.

If these procedures are not carried out, the wings may be prone to splitting or twisting.

7. Still pinching the wing slip firmly in place with the finger and thumb of the left hand, draw the tying silk directly up. The loop of silk between the finger and thumb will compress the wing down onto the hook shank while the same finger and thumb prevent it from twisting out of place and splitting.

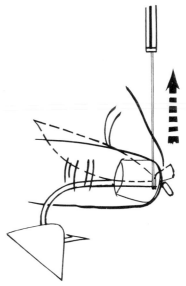

8. Add two or three more turns (tightly) of silk to secure the wing and then trim off the butts. Continue with a few more turns of silk and complete with a whip finish.

9. The finished wing. The tips should sit just proud of the hook bend.

Peter Ross

This famous old wet fly pattern has been chosen for tying at this point because it incorporates many of the techniques covered so far in this book – tying on, forming a body, ribbing, winding a hackle, adding wings (the latest skill) and whip finishing. In the course of tying this fly, pay careful attention to proportions – there is a lot to get onto the hook shank, so make sure enough room remains for adding the wings and forming the whip finished head.

Hook: DE 8–14
Silk: black
Tail: golden pheasant tippets
Body: flat silver tinsel and red seal's fur or wool
Rib: fine oval tinsel (silver)
Hackle: black hen
Wings: teal (breast feather)

1. Begin by tying in a few fibres of golden pheasant tippet for the tail, followed by a length of fine oval tinsel and then a length of flat silver tinsel.

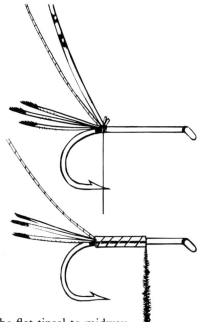

2. Wind the flat tinsel to midway up the shank and tie it in.

3. Now dub a little red seal's fur onto the silk and wind on to complete the body.

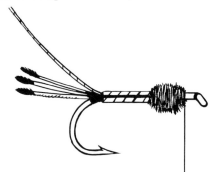

4. Now rib the whole body with even turns of the fine oval tinsel. Tie in and trim off surplus ribbing.

5. Next add a hackle of black hen.

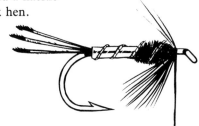

6. Finally tie in the wings, which are made from matched slips of teal breast feather, make a neat head, whip finish and varnish.

Mallard and Claret

Perhaps the most famous of the traditional lake flies, the Mallard and Claret remains enormously popular with stillwater anglers and is a particular favourite of mine, having often produced a fish or two on a day when none of my usual armoury would work!

Hook: DE 8–14
Silk: claret
Tail: golden pheasant tippet fibres
Body: claret seal's fur
Rib: oval gold tinsel or fine gold wire in the smaller sizes
Hackle: dyed claret cock or natural red
Wing: bronze mallard

1. Take the claret tying silk down to the bend and tie in fibres of golden pheasant tippet (up to six) for the tail. Now tie in a length of oval gold tinsel for the rib. Seal's fur dyed claret is now dubbed onto the tying silk.

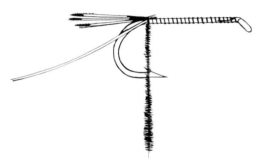

2. Wind the dubbed silk forward to produce a neatly tapered body. Rib the body with even turns of tinsel, tie off and trim the waste.

3. Next, tie in and wind a cock hackle. Moisten the forefinger and thumb and sweep the fibres slightly back (see drawing); a couple of turns of silk will hold it in place.

4. Lastly, the wing of two matched slips of bronze mallard is added. Wind a neat, small head, whip finish and varnish.

Invicta

The beginner may not find the Invicta the easiest of patterns to tie, but dubbing, palmered hackles and wet fly wings – all of which are incorporated in this fly – are techniques which have been covered earlier, so the Invicta might be considered an excellent practice piece as well as a superb catcher of trout.

Hook: DE 8–14
Silk: yellow or black
Tail: golden pheasant crest
Body: yellow seal's fur
Rib: oval gold tinsel
Hackle: red game cock
Wing: hen pheasant centre tail
Throat hackle: blue jay wing fibres

1. Start the waxed tying silk behind the eye and take it down to the bend. Tie in a golden pheasant crest feather for the tail.

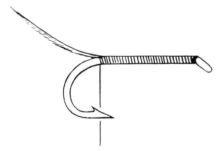

2. Tie in a length of oval gold tinsel and then dub the tying silk with yellow seal's fur.

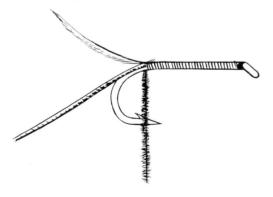

3. Wind up a neat body with the dubbed silk and tie off. Next a hackle feather is tied in at the position shown.

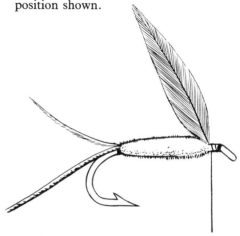

4. The hackle is now wound down the body in wide turns. At the bend trap the hackle tip with the tinsel.

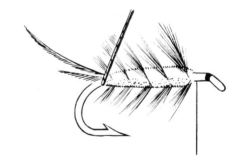

5. The tinsel is now taken in neat turns up the body and through the turns of hackle. Secure the tinsel at the shoulder with the silk and trim waste tinsel. Also trim the hackle tip at the hook bend.

6. Next, two wing slips are cut from a hen pheasant tail, matched together and tied in. Finally, add a throat hackle formed from a bunch of blue jay wing feather fibres. Build up a small head, whip finish and varnish.

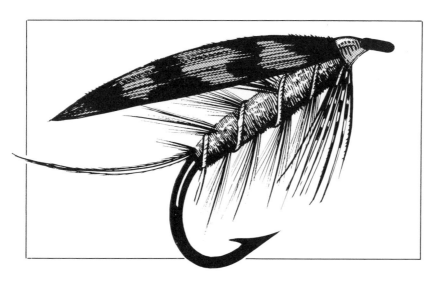

Greenwell's Glory (wet)

If you asked a non-angler to name a fishing fly to you, he would probably think for a moment and then reply 'Greenwell's Glory', such is the fame of this fly.

The product of two men – professional fly dresser James Wright of Sprouston, and the Durham cleric Canon Greenwell – this pattern has over the years become practically immortal.

The body of the fly is shaped with turns of yellow silk which has been well waxed, giving an olive hue to the finished body.

Hook: DE 10–14
Silk: well waxed yellow
Body: as above
Rib: fine gold wire
Hackle: furnace
Wing: blackbird substitute

1. Run the waxed silk down to the bend and there tie in a length of fine gold wire.

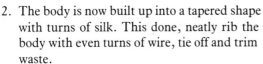

2. The body is now built up into a tapered shape with turns of silk. This done, neatly rib the body with even turns of wire, tie off and trim waste.

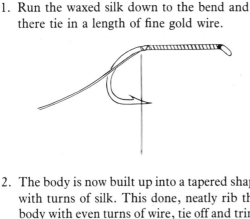

3. A good quality furnace hackle (a red feather with a black centre) is tied in behind the eye and wound in the usual way. Moisten the finger and thumb and sweep the hackles down and hold in position. Take a couple of turns of silk diagonally around the shank to hold the hackle in position.

4. The fly may now be winged with two matching slips of blackbird substitute feather. Wind a neat head, whip finish and varnish.

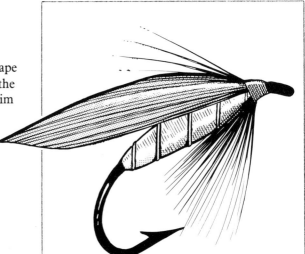

A Hackled Dry Fly

The fly shown in the drawings, the Heron Blue, is typical of the simple hackled dry flies. Although straightforward in its tying, the size of hook used, 14–16, might at first prove troublesome to the beginner, but a little practice will soon produce encouraging results.

Hook: UE 14–16
Silk: grey
Tail whisks: blue-grey cock hackle fibres
Body: three heron herl fibres
Hackle: blue-grey

1. Leaving a little space behind the eye for the winding of the hackle, take the waxed silk down to the bend. First, tie in four or five blue-grey cock hackle fibres to form the tail whisks, and then three fibres of natural heron herl.

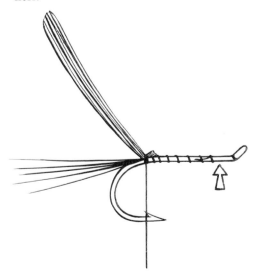

2. Return the silk to the eye and then make a rope of the heron fibres by twisting them together between finger and thumb. Wind the herl up the shank to make the body. Leave space for the hackle. Tie in and trim off waste. Now tie in a blue-grey cock hackle feather.

3. Wind the hackle and then take the tying silk carefully through the turns of hackle to the eye. Build up a neat head with turns of silk, whip finish and varnish.

Split Wings for Dry Flies

The winging of the dry fly follows the same procedure as for the wet fly – two slips are taken from opposing wing feathers and matched together.

In the case of the dry fly, however, the wing slips when placed together must curve outwards, unlike those of the wet fly. As the winging technique requires practice to perfect, I would suggest a morning spent tying wings before progressing to actual patterns.

1. A pair of starling wing feathers, from opposite wings, have slips removed. When placed back to back, the two slips will curve outwards.

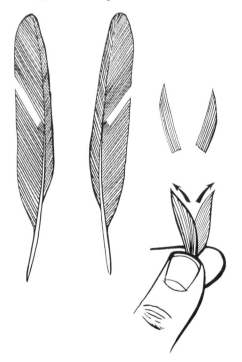

2. Start the waxed silk behind the eye and wind down four or five touching turns to make the 'bed' upon which the wings will sit. Pinching the slips together between finger and thumb, offer up and take two firm turns around the butts.

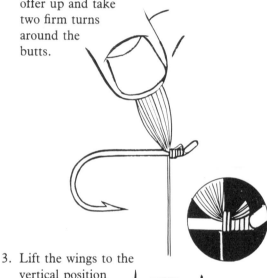

3. Lift the wings to the vertical position and take two turns around the back of the slips.

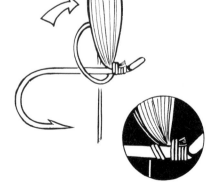

50

4. A turn of silk is passed completely around the base of the feathers.

5. Use the dubbing needle to divide the slips and criss-cross the silk in a figure-of-eight motion to separate them.

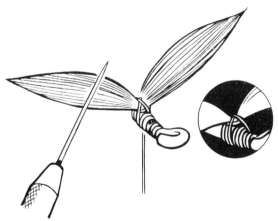

6. The wings are now nicely 'cocked'.

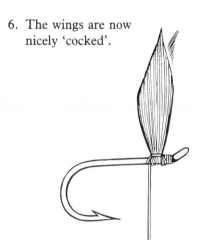

7. 'Advanced wings' are used on the Variant series of dry flies. Initially the slips are tied in with the tips pointing over the hook eye. The remainder of the tying procedure is the same as above. The wings should be held between finger and thumb until the stage shown in No. 5 is reached.

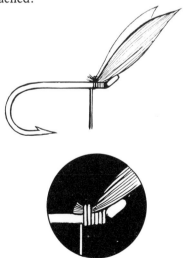

Blue Dun

The Blue Dun is a well-established pattern which incorporates two techniques discussed earlier, dubbing and tying split wings. The dubbing should be applied sparingly to allow the yellow tying silk to 'grin' through when the fly is wet.

Hook: UE 14
Silk: primrose
Tail: fibres taken from a blue dun cock hackle
Body: mole's fur
Wings: starling
Hackle: blue dun cock hackle

1. Take the waxed tying silk down to the bend and catch in three fibres from a blue dun cock hackle to form the tail. Now dub a little mole's fur onto the tying silk.

2. Wind the dubbing up the shank to form a slim tapered body. Prepare the wings to take two slips from opposite wing quills of a starling.

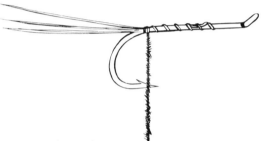

3. Take two or three turns of silk forward to form a 'bed' for the wings and tie them in.

4. Tie in a blue dun cock hackle directly behind the wings.

5. Carefully wind and tie in the hackle, trim off waste, then build up a neat head with turns of silk, whip finish and varnish.

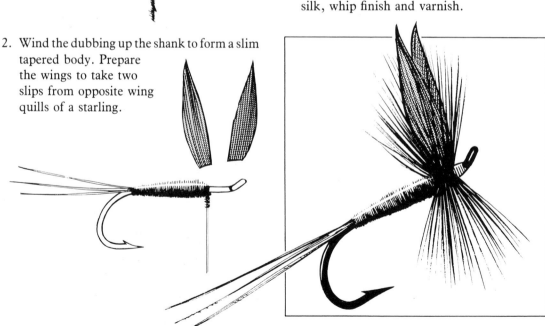

Hackle Point Wings

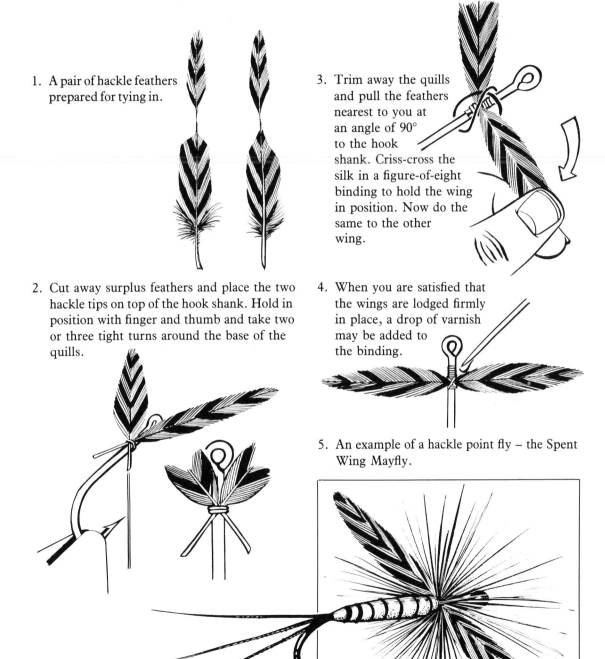

1. A pair of hackle feathers prepared for tying in.

2. Cut away surplus feathers and place the two hackle tips on top of the hook shank. Hold in position with finger and thumb and take two or three tight turns around the base of the quills.

3. Trim away the quills and pull the feathers nearest to you at an angle of 90° to the hook shank. Criss-cross the silk in a figure-of-eight binding to hold the wing in position. Now do the same to the other wing.

4. When you are satisfied that the wings are lodged firmly in place, a drop of varnish may be added to the binding.

5. An example of a hackle point fly – the Spent Wing Mayfly.

Lunn's Particular

Like the insect it was tied to represent – the medium olive spinner – the Lunn's Particular was born and bred on the river Test. The invention of the celebrated river keeper W.J. Lunn, this pattern has accounted for countless numbers of trout since it was originally tied in 1917.

Hook: UE 14–16
Silk: crimson
Tail: four fibres of Rhode Island Red cock hackle
Body: the stripped stalk of a Rhode Island Red hackle
Wings: medium blue dun cock hackle-points
Hackle: Rhode Island Red cock hackle

1. Start the waxed tying silk a little way behind the eye and take it down to the bend. There tie in four fibres from a Rhode Island Red cock hackle. The same feather stripped of its fibres provides the hackle stalk for the body which is now tied in by the thinnest end at the hook bend.

2. Return the silk up the shank and follow up with the hackle stalk, tie in and trim off waste.

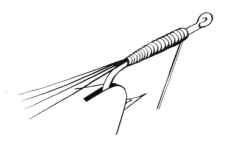

3. Next, a pair of medium blue dun hackle tips are tied in, in the spent position.

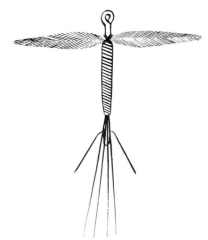

4. Lastly, a stiff Rhode Island Red cock hackle is tied in behind the wings and then carefully wound through them to the eye. Secure the hackle and trim off waste. Build up a neat head with turns of silk, whip finish and varnish.

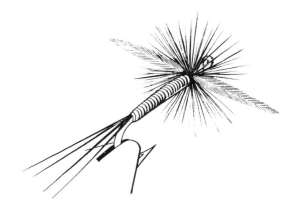

Bunch Wings for Dry Flies

Wings made from bunches of feather offer a simple-to-dress alternative to the conventional split and hackle-point styles of winging.

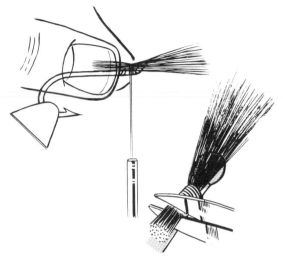

1. Strip away the fibres from the quill of a cock hackle. A moderate sized bunch is required as the fibres will be divided to form wings at a later stage.

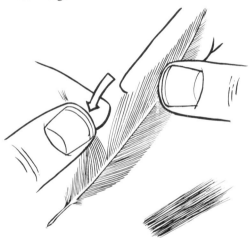

2. Hold the fibres between finger and thumb, offer them up to the hook and check for length. A few turns of silk should be placed behind the eye of the hook to provide a bed upon which the feather fibres will sit. This done, take three or four tight turns around the base of the feathers, taking care to hold them in position with the finger and thumb of the left hand. A spot of varnish may now be added to the binding before proceeding with further turns. When you are satisfied the wing is secure, the feather butts may be trimmed away.

3. The dubbing needle is now used to divide the fibres into two equal sections. Grasp the section nearest to you and draw it round so as to be at right angles to the hook shank.

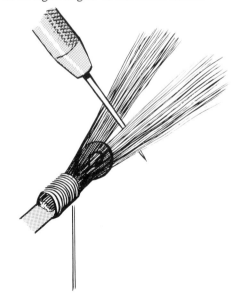

4. The silk is then taken between the wing twice (see dotted line), holding it apart from the remaining bunch of feather. The technique is now repeated with the opposing wing, the silk forming a figure-of-eight binding. A further couple of turns may now be placed immediately in front of the divided wings as shown.

5a. The finished wings.

5b. Close-up view.

Upright wings are simply tied in as a bunch (not divided), raised to the upright position and secured with turns of silk.

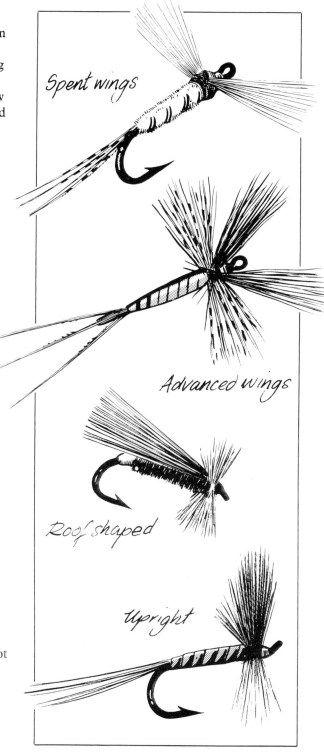

Spent wings

Advanced wings

Roof shaped

Upright

Walker's Sedge

Hook: DE 8–10 long shank
Silk: brown
Body: a tip of arc chrome DF wool, remainder of body three strands of chestnut ostrich herl
Wing: a bunch of red cock hackle fibres
Hackle: two stiff natural red cock hackles

1. Having taken the waxed tying silk down to the bend, catch in a small length of arc chrome DF wool for the butt.

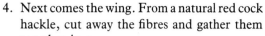

2. Wind the wool forward for a couple of turns, tie off and trim. Next, tie in three fibres of chestnut brown ostrich herl.

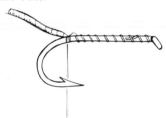

3. Spin the herls together and wind up a body with the herl. Tie off and trim waste. Take your scissors and give the herl a 'haircut', clipping the fibres close to the shank.

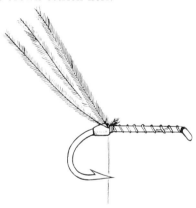

4. Next comes the wing. From a natural red cock hackle, cut away the fibres and gather them together in a bunch. The bunch is now tied in by the fine ends behind the eye.

5. Two natural red cock hackles are now tied in and wound. Trim waste hackles, build up a small head, whip finish and varnish.

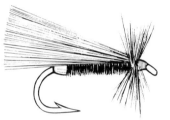

6. Lastly, cut the wing square with the hook bend.

Lures

All trout flies are lures in the strict sense of the word. But when a fly fisherman talks about lures he means the larger-than-average, attractor patterns, possibly designed to imitate small fry, and principally intended for use on still waters. (In fact, a number of the older lures have their origins in patterns that were used to catch sea trout.)

There are some fly tying skills that apply particularly to the dressing of lures, but we begin with a trio that make no new technical demands.

Jersey Herd

Some fly patterns are destined to remain ever green. Tom Ivens' Jersey Herd is typical, a popular lure which figures strongly and throughout the season in the return books of most stillwater trout fisheries I visit.

The body of the original dressing was formed from the foil cap of a milk bottle (hence the name) but to save on your milk bill, substitute flat copper tinsel for the body.

Hook: LS 8–10
Silk: black
Body: floss silk overwound with flat copper tinsel
Tail and back: six fibres of bronze peacock herl
Throat hackle: orange cock hackle fibres

1. Wax the tying silk, start it behind the eye and take it in open turns down to the bend. Tie in a length of flat copper tinsel followed by a length of floss.

2. Select six bronze peacock herls and tie them in leaving about half an inch projecting beyond the bend to form a tail. Return the silk to the eye.

3. A neat tapering body is now wound with the floss. Tie off and trim waste floss.

4. Now wind the copper tinsel over the floss body, tie off and trim waste. A hot orange cock hackle is now tied in and wound.

5. Gather the peacock herls together and stretch them over the back of the fly. Secure with two or three tight turns of silk.

6. The remaining herl is twisted between the finger and thumb into a rope and wound round the hook shank twice to form a bushy head. Tie off and trim waste. Build up a small head, whip finish and varnish. Lastly, trim the tail fibres square.

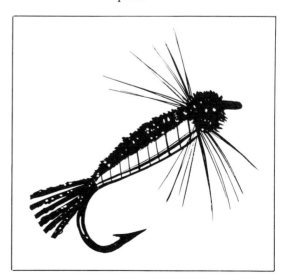

The Missionary

The Missionary is an old pattern made popular by Northampton's Dick Shrive. It has accounted for thousands of stillwater trout and is well worthy of a place in the fly wallet.

Hook: DE 8–10 long shank
Silk: black
Tail: scarlet cock hackle feathers
Body: white chenille
Rib: flat silver tinsel
Throat hackle: scarlet cock hackle fibres
Wing: whole silver mallard breast feather

1. Wind the silk down to the bend and tie in a bunch of scarlet cock hackle fibres.

2. This is followed by a length of silver tinsel and a length of white chenille. Return the silk to the eye.

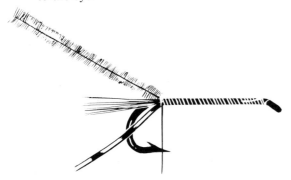

3. Wind the chenille up the shank to the eye and tie in. Trim off the waste.

4. Follow up with the tinsel rib. Tie in and trim.

5. Now tie in the throat hackle using the same material as for the tail.

6. Finally, tie in a whole silver mallard breast feather by the quill to lay flat on top of the body. This acts like a parachute, slowing the fly's descent through the water.

Baby Doll (Variation)

The tying instructions for the Baby Doll given below differ from the original pattern only in respect of the body. I much prefer to build up a tapered, fish-shaped body with turns of wool, as I believe it adds realism, particularly when the fly is retrieved slowly.

Hook: LS 6–10
Silk: black
Body: white Sirdar brand baby wool
Tail: as body

1. Prepare the hook by giving it a coat of varnish which will help prevent the white wool being discoloured by iron stain.

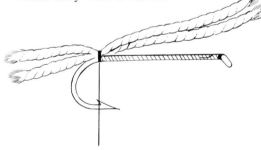

2. Take the black tying silk down to the bend and there tie in two lengths of white Sirdar brand baby wool as shown.

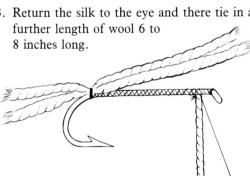

3. Return the silk to the eye and there tie in a further length of wool 6 to 8 inches long.

4. The wool is now wound evenly down to the bend and then returned up the shank forming a nicely tapered body. Tie off behind the eye and trim waste.

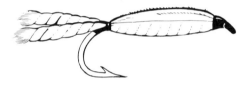

5. The two lengths of wool tied in initially are now pulled down over the back of the fly and secured behind the eye with turns of silk. Trim waste wool and build up a head with turns of silk. Whip finish and varnish.

6. Remove the hook from the vice and with your dubbing needle thoroughly shred the two sections of wool hanging over the hook and bend into a bushy tail.

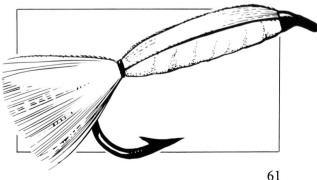

Hair Wings for Lures

Hair wings are simple to tie and yet remain extremely durable. Common furs in use include bucktail, squirrel, goat, bear and skunk. A useful tip when tying hair wings for lures, or indeed any lure in the 6–8 hook size class, is to step up the strength of the silk. I use fine-gauge rod-whipping silk.

1. Cut away a bunch of hair close to the skin. Aim for approximately one eighth of an inch when compressed between finger and thumb.

2. With the finger and thumb of the right hand offer up the wing to the hook and check for length. Trim away excess hair (dotted line).

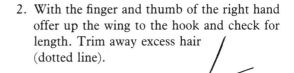

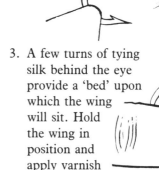

3. A few turns of tying silk behind the eye provide a 'bed' upon which the wing will sit. Hold the wing in position and apply varnish or glue to the wing root and then tie in with firm turns of silk.

4. Build up a neatly tapered head.

5. A couple of turns of silk taken behind the wing root will raise the wing slightly if desired. Return the silk to the head, whip finish and varnish.

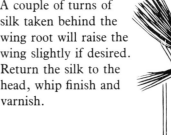

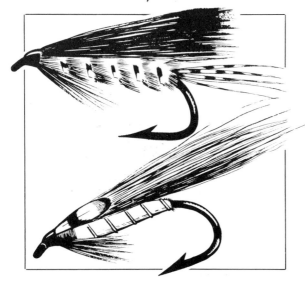

Sweeny Todd

Developed by Dick Walker and Pete Thomas in the mid-sixties, the Sweeny Todd has become one of the most popular of reservoir lures.

I remember fishing from a boat at Powdermill reservoir and taking eleven perch followed by four rainbows all on consecutive casts with a Sweeny Todd.

It is a simple pattern to dress but has none the less suffered 'improvements' over the years. The original dressing is given here.

Hook: DE 6–12 long shank
Body: black floss with a collar of magenta DRF wool
Rib: fine silver wire
Wing: black squirrel tail
Throat hackle: dyed crimson cock hackle fibres
Silk: black

1. Take the waxed silk down to the bend, and tie in a length of fine silver wire and a length of black floss.

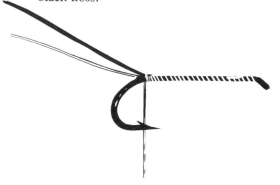

2. Wind the floss up the shank and tie in. Follow this with the wire, forming a neat rib. Trim off waste and catch in a short length of magenta DRF wool and then wind it around the shank two or three times to form a collar.

3. Add a bunch of dyed crimson cock hackle fibres to form the throat hackle.

4. Finally, add the wing, which is made from a bunch of black squirrel tail fibres; wind a neat head with the tying silk, and whip finish, and varnish.

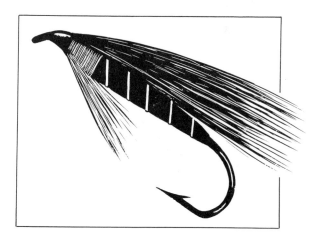

Royal Coachman Bucktail

This is a lure that originated in the United States where it has been developed from the more traditional coachman pattern.

Hook: DE 6–10 long shank
Silk: black
Tail: three fibres of golden pheasant tippets
Butt: two fibres of peacock herl
Body: crimson floss
Throat hackle: bunch of black cock hackle fibres
Wing: white bucktail

1. Take the waxed tying silk down to the bend of the hook and catch in three golden pheasant tippets.

2. Follow this with two lengths of peacock herl and a length of scarlet floss.

3. Twist the peacock herls together and wind around the shank two or three times to make the butt. Tie in and trim off waste herl.

4. Add a throat hackle of black cock hackle fibres.

5. Finally, tie in the wing, made from a bunch of white bucktail fibres.

Deer Hair Spinning

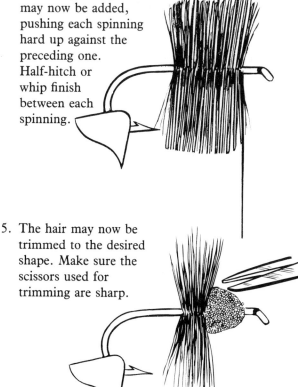

It was Don Gapen's now famous Muddler Minnow pattern which first introduced UK anglers to the uses of deer hair. Spun in bunches along the hook shank, the fur may then be clipped to any desired shape and has the advantage of being both very light and extremely buoyant.

The following points should be borne in mind when tying deer hair. Use a stronger grade of silk than normal – I would recommend fine rod whipping silk; deer hair may only be spun effectively on a bare hook; and use only sharp scissors for the final trimming.

Cut off a bunch of hair from the base of the skin (approximately one eighth of an inch when compressed).

1. Place the bunch of hair on top of the hook shank.

2. Take a couple of loose turns of silk around the deer hair and hook shank.

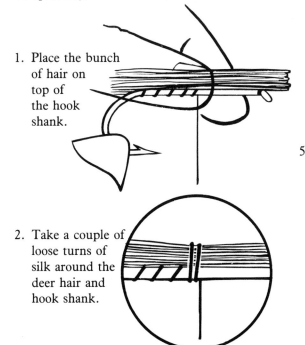

3. Pull down firmly on the tying silk and keep under tension. The fur spins around the shank. Wind the silk through the spinning of fur and secure with a half-hitch or whip finish.

4. Further spinnings of fur may now be added, pushing each spinning hard up against the preceding one. Half-hitch or whip finish between each spinning.

5. The hair may now be trimmed to the desired shape. Make sure the scissors used for trimming are sharp.

Muddler Minnow

Hook: LS 6–12
Silk: black fine-gauge rod-whipping silk
Tail: bronze turkey
Body: flat gold tinsel
Underwing: natural squirrel tail fibres
Wing: bronze turkey
Head: deer hair

1. Cut two pairs of matching slips from left and right wing feathers of a natural bronze turkey and place them to one side. Fix a long shank hook in the vice.

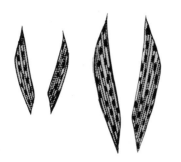

2. Starting the black tying silk a little way behind the eye, continue in open turns down to the bend. Match the smaller feather slips together and tie them in to form a tail. Now tie in a length of flat gold tinsel.

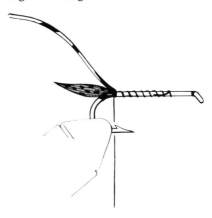

3. Wind the tinsel forward and tie in at the position shown.

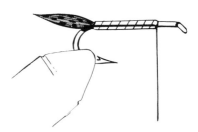

4. An underwing of natural squirrel tail fibres is now added.

5. The larger wing slips are now tied over the squirrel tail fibres.

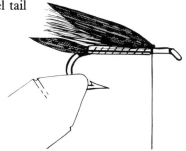

6. The final stage in the dressing is the head made from spinnings of deer hair. Cut a pinch of deer hair from close to the skin and offer it up to the hook with the cut ends pointing over the eye. Take a couple of loose turns around the fibres with the silk.

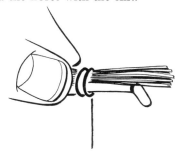

7. Hold the fur in position with the left hand. Now pull down firmly on the silk. The fur will stand out at right angles to the hook shank.

8. Take the silk through the fur and secure it with a half-hitch or whip finish. A further spinning of fur may now be added to butt up to the first. The difference with the second and any subsequent spinnings is that the left hand holding the fur in position releases its grip as the right hand pulls on the silk, allowing the whole bunch to flare and revolve around the hook shank.

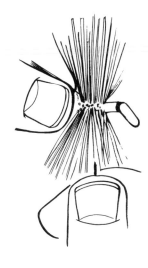

9. The silk is then taken through the fur to the eye and secured with a varnished whip finish. The head may now be clipped to the rounded muddler shape with sharp scissors.

Streamer Wings

Made from strips of feather or more commonly a matched pair or pairs of whole hackles, streamer lures are both elegant and straightforward to dress. The drawings show a simple streamer wing made from badger cock hackles – a white feather with a black centre.

1. Two matching badger cock hackles ready for tying in.

2. Place the feathers together (pattern side out) and offer up to the hook for length. Streamer wings are normally tied one and a half to two times the hook length.

3. Grip the wing with the finger and thumb of the left hand and hold in position. Take three or four tight turns around the feather butts. Check that the wing is sitting squarely and then make a further few tight turns. Trim off feather butts and build up a neat tapered head and whip finish.

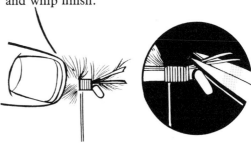

4. Although the illustration depicts wings tied with a single pair of feathers, two, three or even four pairs may be used and are tied in exactly the same way.

A selection of streamer lures

Jack Frost

Designed and popularized by Bob Church, the Jack Frost lure has achieved some remarkable results. A useful tip passed on to me by London angler Albie Mew is thoroughly to wet marabou lures prior to casting; this saves the delicate fibres from being broken up when false casting.

Hook: LS 6–10
Silk: black or white
Tail: red wool
Body: white wool overwrapped with clear polythene
Wing: white marabou
Hackles: crimson cock and white

1. Take the waxed tying silk down to the bend and tie in a tuft of red wool for the tail.

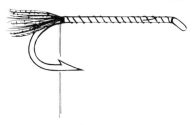

2. A length of polythene sheeting approximately one eighth of an inch wide is tied in, followed by a length of white wool (Sirdar brand baby wool).

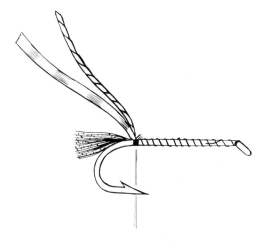

3. The wool is now wound forward and tied off behind the eye. Trim waste wool. The whole body is now overwrapped with the polythene sheeting, which is then tied off and trimmed.

4. Next, the wing made from a generous spray of white marabou is added.

5. Tie in first a large crimson cock hackle followed by a natural white cock hackle. Wind each hackle in turn, tie off and trim. Build up a largish head, whip finish and varnish.

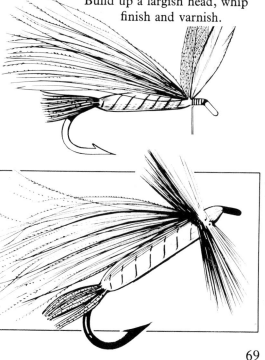

Some Other Patterns

Montana Stone

As the name suggests, the Montana Stone is an American pattern and one which has become a favourite of mine, particularly at the beginning of the season.

Hook: DE 10–12 long shank
Silk: black
Tail: black cock hackle fibres
Body: rear – black chenille, front – yellow chenille
Hackle: soft black hen

1. Starting behind the eye, carry the silk down to the bend and tie in a small bunch of black cock hackle fibres to form the tail. Now tie in a length of black chenille.

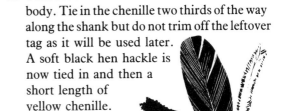

2. Take the silk forward and wind in the chenille body. Tie in the chenille two thirds of the way along the shank but do not trim off the leftover tag as it will be used later. A soft black hen hackle is now tied in and then a short length of yellow chenille.

3. Wind the yellow chenille forward, tie it in and trim off waste. The hackle is now wound forward Palmer style and tied in.

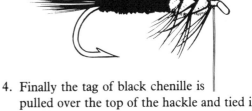

4. Finally the tag of black chenille is pulled over the top of the hackle and tied in. With turns of silk, build up a generous head, whip finish and then varnish.

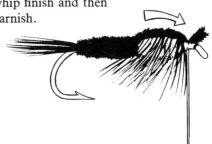

Black Matuka

Hook: DE 6–10 long shank
Silk: black
Wing: two matching black hen hackles
Body: black chenille
Rib: oval silver tinsel
Throat hackle: black cock hackle fibres

1. Select two identical black hen hackles and prepare them by stripping away the fluffy fibres at the base of each feather. This done, place them to one side.

2. Fix a long shank hook in the vice and run waxed tying silk down to the bend. Now tie in a length of oval silver tinsel, followed by a length of black chenille. Return the silk to the eye and wind up a neat chenille body. Do not rib the body at this stage.

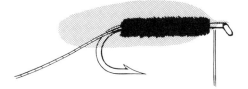

3. Place the two hackle feathers together with the shiny sides facing outwards, offer them up to the hook and check for length. Allow approximately a third of the feathers to stand proud of the hook bend.

4. Gripping the feathers tightly together strip away two thirds of the underside fibres with the forefinger and thumb. The prepared wing should then resemble this drawing.

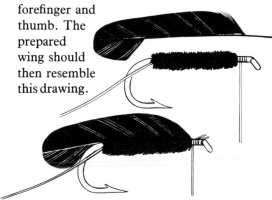

5. Holding the wing in position, tie it in by the feather butts.

6. The feather fibres are now divided by stroking them forward. The rib is then taken through them and around the body in the normal manner. Stroke the fibres back into position and repeat the procedure, working up the hook shank to the eye. Tie in the rib with the silk and trim off waste. A bunch of black cock hackle fibres may now be added at this stage to form the beard or throat hackle. Build up the head with turns of silk, whip finish and varnish.

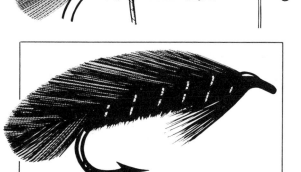

The Perrin-Mew

Originally tied by South London angler Albie Mew and developed with a friend Joe Perrin, the Perrin-Mew lure has chalked up an impressive record over two seasons. Dick Walker has suggested that a new pattern should not be 'launched' until it has accounted for at least fifty trout. Apart from many many limit bags, this lure has given Joe Perrin a rainbow of 8 lb 10 oz, and myself a five-fish limit with a total weight of 21 lb 15 oz.

Hook: the original pattern was dressed on a standard shank but long shanks may be used, size 6–8.
Silk: black
Tail: black marabou
Rib: flat silver tinsel
Body: dubbed marabou fibres
Wing cases: white marabou
Throat hackle: white marabou

1. A black marabou plume. The long spiky fibres (shown above the dotted line) are used for the tail whereas the fibres below are used for dubbing the body of the fly.

2. Take the black tying silk down to the bend and there tie in a generous spray of marabou cut from the top section of the feather. A length of flat silver tinsel is now tied in.

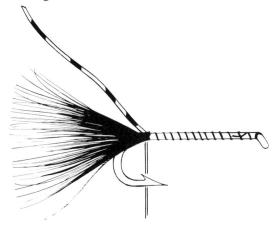

3. From a bottom section of the marabou plume, cut away a bunch of fibres and break them up between your fingers and thumbs.

4. Dub the silk with the fibres and wind it forward to the point shown on the drawing. Follow up with a neat tinsel rib. Tie off and trim.

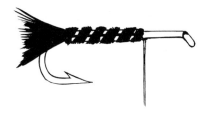

5. A bunch of white marabou is now tied in as shown and then a little more black dubbing is applied to the silk and wound forward.

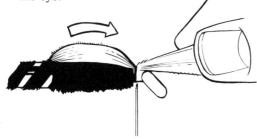

6. Gather the white marabou into a bunch, stretch it forward and secure with silk behind the eye.

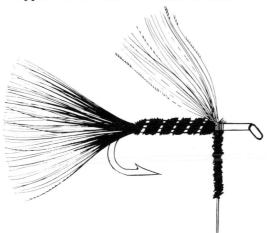

7. The white marabou, which is now facing forward, should be separated into two equal bunches and divided with the silk in a figure of eight binding.

8. Now bring the fibres down on either side of the body and pull them slightly back. Hold them in position and build up a neat head with turns of silk. Whip finish.

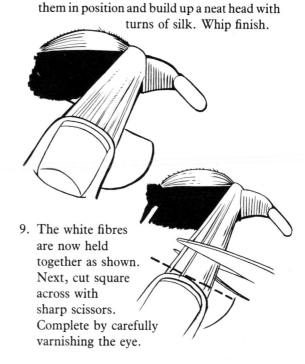

9. The white fibres are now held together as shown. Next, cut square across with sharp scissors. Complete by carefully varnishing the eye.

Special Bodies

In the following three sections are described some alternative materials and techniques for constructing fly bodies.

Latex

Latex, one of the most versatile of the new materials for fly bodies, is supplied in sheet form of various thickness. The four flies illustrated demonstrate the versatility of latex:

(a) Midge Pupa

(b) Freshwater Shrimp. The olive tinted latex is tied in at the hook bend, stretched over the body and secured at the head. The body is then ribbed with 2 lb clear monofil

(c) Dragon fly nymph (*Zygopterid*)

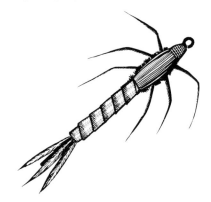

(d) The artificial of the Giant Stonefly nymph. This spectacular creature, over 2 inches long, is a native of the USA and has a rather complicated structure of wing cases. American fly dresser Paul Jorgensen uses latex to copy the wing cases and to provide the ribbing on the body

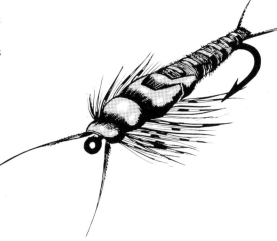

1. Use a straight edge and a pencil to mark the latex to size then cut it into strips. I use a scalpel for this but straight-bladed scissors are equally good.

2. Trim one end of the strip into a point.

3. Natural latex is buffish fawn in colour – a shade that suits a number of insects' bodies. Should a specific colour be required, however, felt marker pens (waterproof) are ideal.

4. Tie in the strip by the pointed end. At this stage, an underbody of floss or wool may be added if desired.

underbody

5. Wind the latex forward, slightly overlapping each turn. Tie off and trim. The finished body closely resembles the natural segmentation common to many insects.

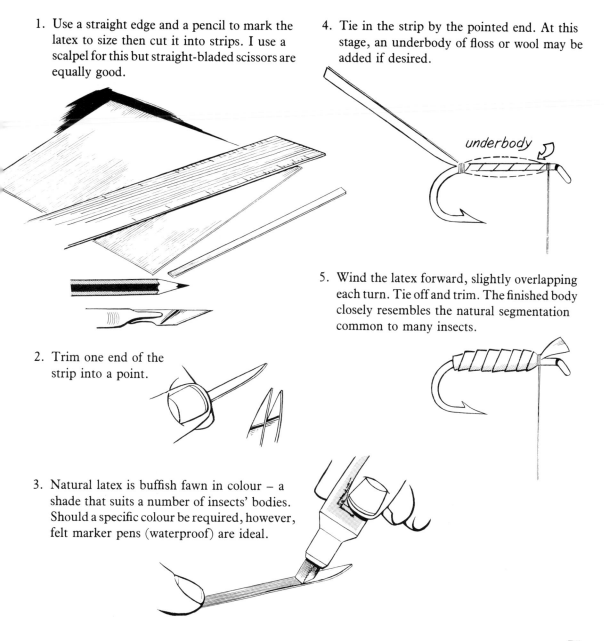

Peacock Quill

A herl taken from the 'eye' section of the peacock's tail feather and stripped of its flue is used for the bodies of many traditional dry fly patterns.

The prepared quill has a beautiful dual marking of black merging into a buffish grey which, when wound up the hook shank, represents the segments of the natural fly's body.

1. From the eye section of the feather remove a herl.

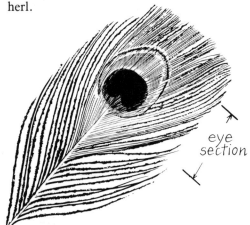

eye section

A quill bodied dry fly – the Ginger Quill

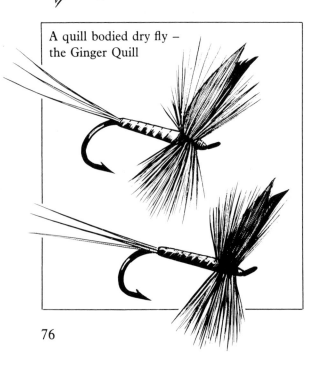

2. Place the herl on a flat surface and gently remove the flue – the short feather fibres on the quill. For this job I find an artist's putty rubber is ideal although a penknife or even the finger and thumbnails may be used. Work carefully – the quill is very delicate.

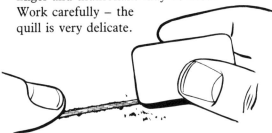

3. Prepared quills with their light and dark markings. Some fly patterns call for a quill body of a specific colour and for this I would suggest waterproof felt marker pens be used.

4. Place a hook in the vice and run the waxed tying silk down to the bend in touching turns. This provides a foundation over which the quill is later wound. The quill is now tied in with the darker section facing toward the band. Return the silk up the shank. Now carefully wind the quill up the shank, taking care not to overlap each turn. Tie in and trim off waste and the quill body is complete.

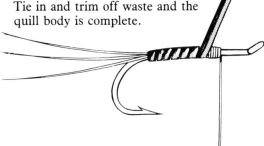

Swannundaze

Swannundaze is the unusual brand name given to a plastic fly body material imported by Veniards from the United States. Designed to represent the segmented bodies common to a wide variety of insects, this plastic strip is flat on one side and rounded on the other. When wound on the hook shank it looks most realistic.

Swannundaze is sold in a variety of colours, including transparent, and my drawing shows a selection of nymphs incorporating this material.

1. With sharp scissors cut a length of Swannundaze and trim one end to a point as shown.

2. The point should then be scored slightly to give a purchase to the tying silk when the material is initially tied in. This can be done with a penknife or more simply by nibbling the end of the plastic with your teeth.

3. Tie in the Swannundaze as shown.

4. Wind up the hook shank, tie off and trim.

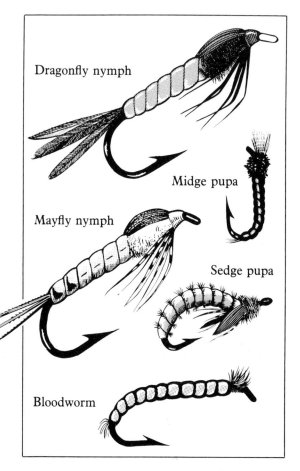

Dragonfly nymph

Midge pupa

Mayfly nymph

Sedge pupa

Bloodworm

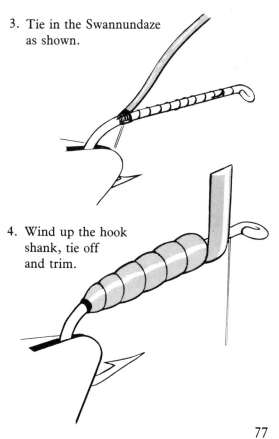

Special Patterns

There now follows a sequence of sections devoted to the tying of some less conventional patterns, involving materials and techniques that are generally peculiar to the patterns under construction.

Caddis Larvae

Unlike the snail which carries its home upon its back, the larvae of some species of sedge or caddis flies go one better. A case composed of minute pebbles or leaf fragments, twigs, etc., is built to completely envelop the body, leaving only the head and legs visible.

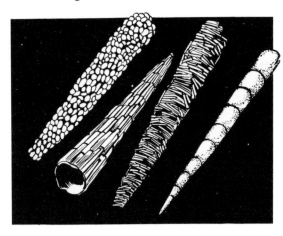

Anyone who has ever paused to examine examples of caddis cases can only marvel at the intricacy of their construction job.

Hook: LS 8–12
Silk: tan, green or brown
Body: wool or floss coated in glue and then covered with fine clean gravel or strips of raffia
Hackle: small brown cock hackle tied sparsely

1. Run the waxed tying silk down to the bend and tie in a length of wool or floss. Return the silk to the eye and wind up a neat tapered body with the wool or floss, tie off and trim waste.

2. Use a matchstick as a spatula and thoroughly coat the body of the fly with adhesive. (I would recommend five-minute epoxy glue.)

3. Small particles of gravel are sprinkled over the glued floss until the body is completely covered. Alternatively, strips of raffia in shades of brown and green may be used. When the body is dry, a small sparse hackle is added, imitating the legs of the larvae. Build up a head with turns of silk, whip finish and varnish.

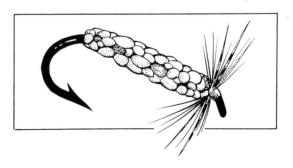

Daddy Longlegs

The first stage in the dressing of the 'daddy' is to prepare the legs. These are made from six fibres taken from a cock pheasant tail. Knot each fibre once in the middle and when you have prepared all six, place them to one side.

Hook: LS 10–12
Silk: brown
Body: three fibres of bronze turkey wing (or substitute)
Legs: six fibres of cock pheasant tail
Wings: ginger hackle-points
Hackle: natural red

1. At the bend tie in three fibres from a bronze turkey wing (or substitute).

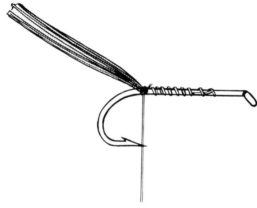

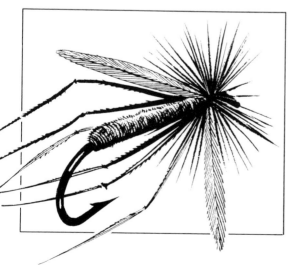

2. By twisting them together make a rope of the fibres and wind them forward to form the insect's body. Tie in and trim off waste.

3. The legs are now tied in as shown. Note that the legs should trail back as in the drawing and not spread all around the insect.

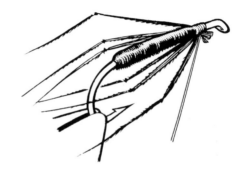

4. Two ginger hackle tips are now tied in to make the wings. These should not be tied at 90° to the shank, but swept back a little.

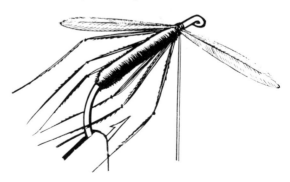

5. Finally, add a natural red cock hackle, wind a neat head with the silk, whip finish and varnish.

Floating Snail

Hook: 10–14
Silk: black
Body: cork overwound
with stripped bronze
green peacock herl

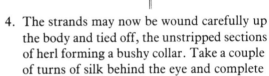

1. Using a scalpel and an emery board, cut and shape a piece of cork. The finished body should appear as below, pear-shaped with a flat top. Once this is done, cut a groove down the length of the body and halfway through.

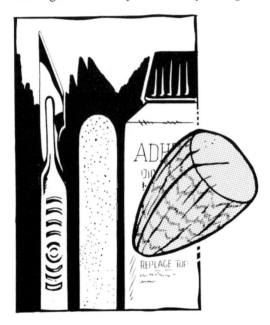

2. The cork is then securely glued to the hook shank.

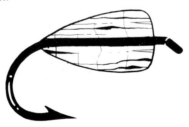

3. While the body dries, proceed to the next stage. From two strands of bronze peacock, strip away the herl, leaving only a third of it remaining. The two strands are now tied in by the stripped ends at the hook bend.

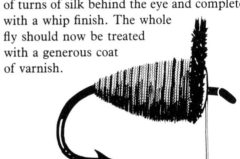

4. The strands may now be wound carefully up the body and tied off, the unstripped sections of herl forming a bushy collar. Take a couple of turns of silk behind the eye and complete with a whip finish. The whole fly should now be treated with a generous coat of varnish.

5. The finished floating snail.

Popper Lure

While it would be an exaggeration to say that the American-originated surface-running lures and poppers have a huge following in the UK, there has in fact been a growing interest shown in the dressing (and fishing) of these patterns in recent years.

Just what these creations are meant to represent is debatable, but the fact remains that the popper patterns can often prove very effective, particularly on the days of flat calm.

Hook: LS 8–10
Tail: large spray of marabou
Body: shaped cork

1. Cut a pear-shaped piece of cork. The flat surface of the cork should then be sanded into a concave shape.

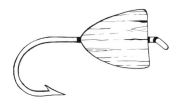

2. Cut a slit the length of the cork and glue the section to the shank of a no. 8 lure hook. Having tried a range of adhesives, I still prefer the five-minute epoxy variety.

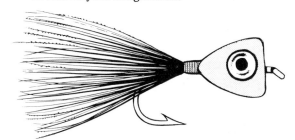

3. Paint the cork with enamel or coloured Vycoat. Add eye detail. When the body is dry, tie in a good spray of marabou for the tail. The variations of colour schemes can be as wide as your imagination.

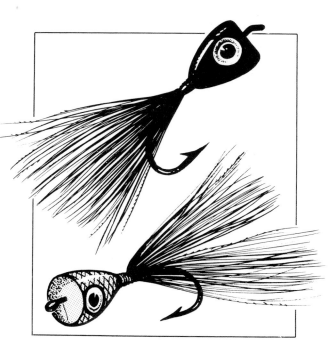

Damosel Wiggle Nymph

Hook: DE 8–12
Silk: brown
Tail: three olive cock hackle tips
Body: olive seal's fur
Rib: flat silver tinsel
Thorax: dark olive seal's fur
Wing cases: dyed brown turkey tail
Legs: olive cock hackle

1. Run the waxed tying silk down to the bend and there tie in three olive cock hackle strips for the tail. Follow this with a length of flat silver tinsel for the rib. The silk is now dabbed with olive seal's fur.

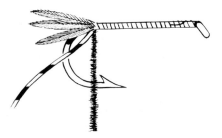

2. Wind the dubbed fur up the shank into a tapering body, then neatly rib the body with the tinsel and trim waste. Whip finish and varnish.

3. Take the hook from the vice and with wire cutters remove the bend and point close to tail.

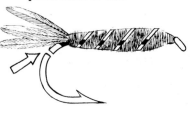

4. A fresh hook is placed in the vice and a tippet of either fuse wire or monofil is whipped on the top of the shank, leaving a section proud of the hook bend.

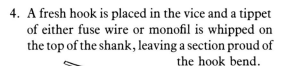

5. Thread the completed tail section through the hook eye on to the monofil tippet which is now pulled down and lashed to the hook shank.

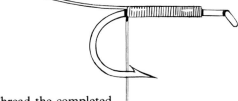

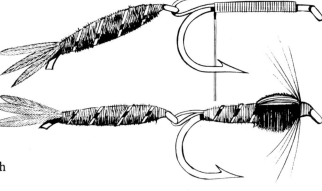

6. The remainder of the dressing may now be completed using olive seal's fur for the body with a darker shade for the thorax. (Do not forget the silver rib on the body.) The wing cases of the original dressing call for dyed brown turkey tail fibres doubled and redoubled over the thorax. Finally tie in a bunch of olive cock hackle fibres or one turn of olive hackle to imitate the legs. Build up a head with turns of silk, whip finish and varnish.

Prisma Fry

The Prisma Fry pattern incorporates a shiny reflective plastic sheeting known as Prismatic. Cut into strips and tied along the hook shank, this material gives a beautiful flash when it is worked through the water, typical of the tiny fish that this fly represents.

When this feature was first published I received a number of inquiries from readers who had experienced difficulty in obtaining Prismatic. I referred them to Veniards and I have heard nothing since!

Hook: LS 6–10
Silk: black
Tail: bunch of white cock hackle fibres
Body: white wool
Cheeks: Prismatic plastic
Wing: dyed black skunk or squirrel tail
Throat hackle: same as tail

1. Cut from the Prismatic sheeting two strips approximately the length of the hook by one eighth of an inch wide. Trim the strips as indicated by the dotted lines on the drawing and place them to one side.

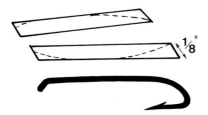

2. Fix the hook in the vice and run tying silk down to the bend. Tie in firmly a generous bunch of white cock hackle fibres for the tail and then clip them square as shown. Now tie in a length of plain white wool.

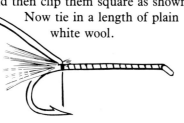

3. Wind the wool up the shank, tie off and trim.

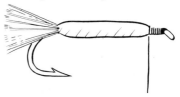

4. Now tie in the Prismatic strips, one on either side of the wool body.

5. The wing, formed from a bunch of black skunk or squirrel hair, is now added, followed by the throat hackle. Build up a largish head with turns of silk, whip finish and varnish.

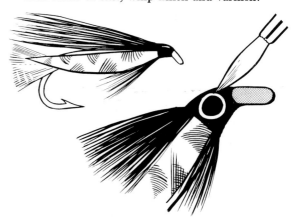

This fry, along with a great many 'fry' patterns, is improved immeasurably by the addition of painted eyes. It takes only a few seconds to do and is well worth the effort.

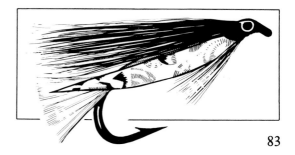

Girdle Bug

There may be stranger looking 'flies' than the American girdle bug, but I cannot think of many off hand. Despite its odd appearance, this attractor pattern, equipped with waving tail and legs, can prove deadly when fished slowly along the bottom. The original dressing, shown here, gives a black body, but green, brown and white are useful variations.

Hook: LS 8–10
Silk: black
Tail and legs: trimmed white elastic bands
Body: black chenille

1. The tail and legs are made from thin white elastic bands trimmed to length. Begin by cutting a whole band in half, one half of which will form the tail section. A further three strips are then cut for the legs.

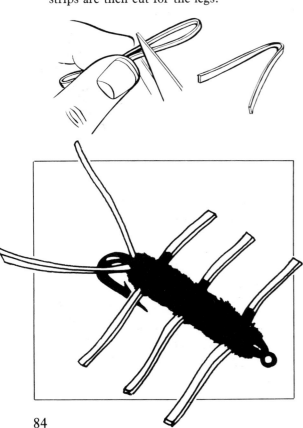

2. Place a no. 8 or 10 long shank hook in the vice and run the waxed tying silk down to the bend. Tie in the tail section of elastic band at the bend with a figure-of-eight binding, then tie in a length of black chenille immediately above the tail. The legs are now secured with a figure-of-eight binding at equal distances up the hook shank.

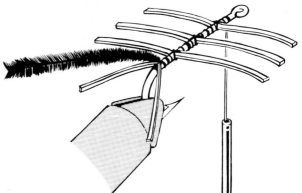

3. The chenille is then wound up to the eye and secured with the silk. Trim off waste chenille and build up a head with turns of silk. Whip finish and varnish.

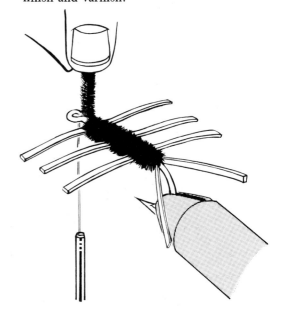

Odds and Sundries

The Eyes Have It!

The addition of a pair of eyes greatly enhances the appearance of many nymphs and lures. They may be simply painted on to the head of the fly, or tied in as a separate part of the dressing.

The eyes shown in the drawing are made from a section of chain. You will have seen the sort I mean attached to pens and used to restrain absentminded bank customers from wandering off with the bank's property. There is a slightly less risky source of supply, namely the cheap keyring type of chain which may be bought for a few pence at many newsagents.

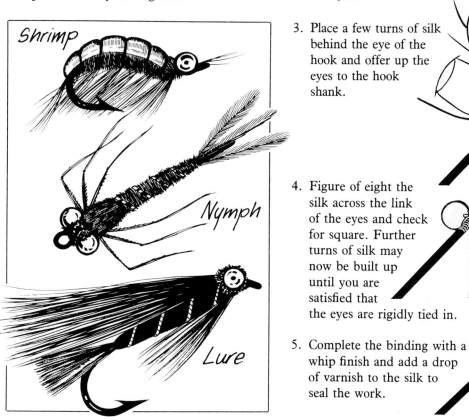

Shrimp

Nymph

Lure

1. Using an old pair of scissors or, better still, small wire cutters, cut away a pair of eyes from the chain.

3. Place a few turns of silk behind the eye of the hook and offer up the eyes to the hook shank.

4. Figure of eight the silk across the link of the eyes and check for square. Further turns of silk may now be built up until you are satisfied that the eyes are rigidly tied in.

5. Complete the binding with a whip finish and add a drop of varnish to the silk to seal the work.

Raffene Spinner Wings

Many fly dressers will be familiar with Raffene, the brand name given to a synthetic raffia used in such famous patterns as the Polystickle and Chomper series of flies. The making of spinner wings from this versatile material is a lesser known technique.

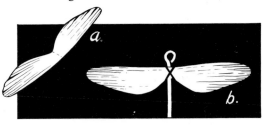

1. Cut a length of Raffene approximately 1½ inches long.

2. Carefully unroll the Raffene and smooth it flat on a hard surface.

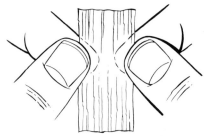

3. Now fold the section in half. With sharp scissors, cut out the wing shape (indicated by the dotted line).

4a. The prepared wings.

4b. The wings tied in with figure-of-eight winding of silk.

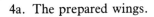

The wings may now be given a thin coat of varnish (Vycoat), which will make them water repellent and durable as well as imparting a realistic transparency. Westerham professional Taff Price ties an unvarnished spinner wing which, when cast, soon becomes waterlogged, closely imitating the drowned spinner.

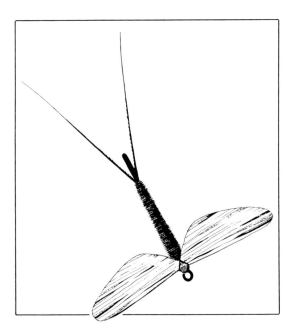

Speciality Hooks

It is due largely to the efforts of progressive hook manufacturers such as Partridges of Redditch, that fly dressers have such an excellent range of speciality hooks to choose from. The five shown below are by no means the whole range currently in production, but will demonstrate the varying application of such hooks.

1. Designed to represent the nymph in a free-swimming posture, the Veniard hook is ideal for such artificials as the dragonfly nymph shown in the drawing.

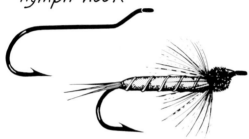

John Veniard swimming nymph hook

2. The Yorkshire firm of Mackenzie-Philips designed and market the Yorkshire sedge hook, the curve of the shank resembling the natural curvature of a number of nymphs. My drawing shows the midge pupa (top) and sedge pupa (below).

Yorkshire sedge hook

3. The ingenious flybody hook, again from Mackenzie-Philips, provides the means of tying extremely realistic dry flies, the bend and point of the hook being masked with turns of hackle.

Yorkshire flybody hook

4. Swedish fly fishermen Nils Eriksson and Gunnar Jahnson developed the Swedish dry fly hook. The wings and hackle are secured on the vertical pillar.

Swedish dry fly hook

5. New Zealand fly dresser Keith Draper
   designed this double-shanked hook to imitate
   the basic shape of many of the flat-bodied
   nymphs. The drawing shows a pattern of my
   own to imitate the larvae of the great diving
   beetle (*Dytiscus marginalis*).

Draper hook

Recommended Reading

Fly Tying for Beginners, Geoffrey Bucknall
(Ernest Benn £3.95)
Fly Tying Techniques, Jaqueline Wakeford
(Ernest Benn £9.95)

Fly Dressing Materials, John Veniard (A & C
Black £9.50)
Taff Price's Still Water Flies, Books 1, 2 and 3,
Taff Price (Ernest Benn £5.75, £6.95, £5.95)

Index